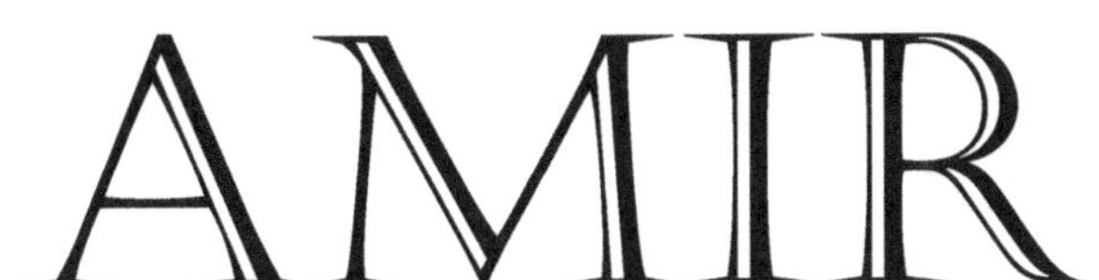 

Amir Kazzaz is a freelance artist who loves character design, all illustrative work, and their pet snake. You see more of their work at amirkazzazportfolio.carrd.com

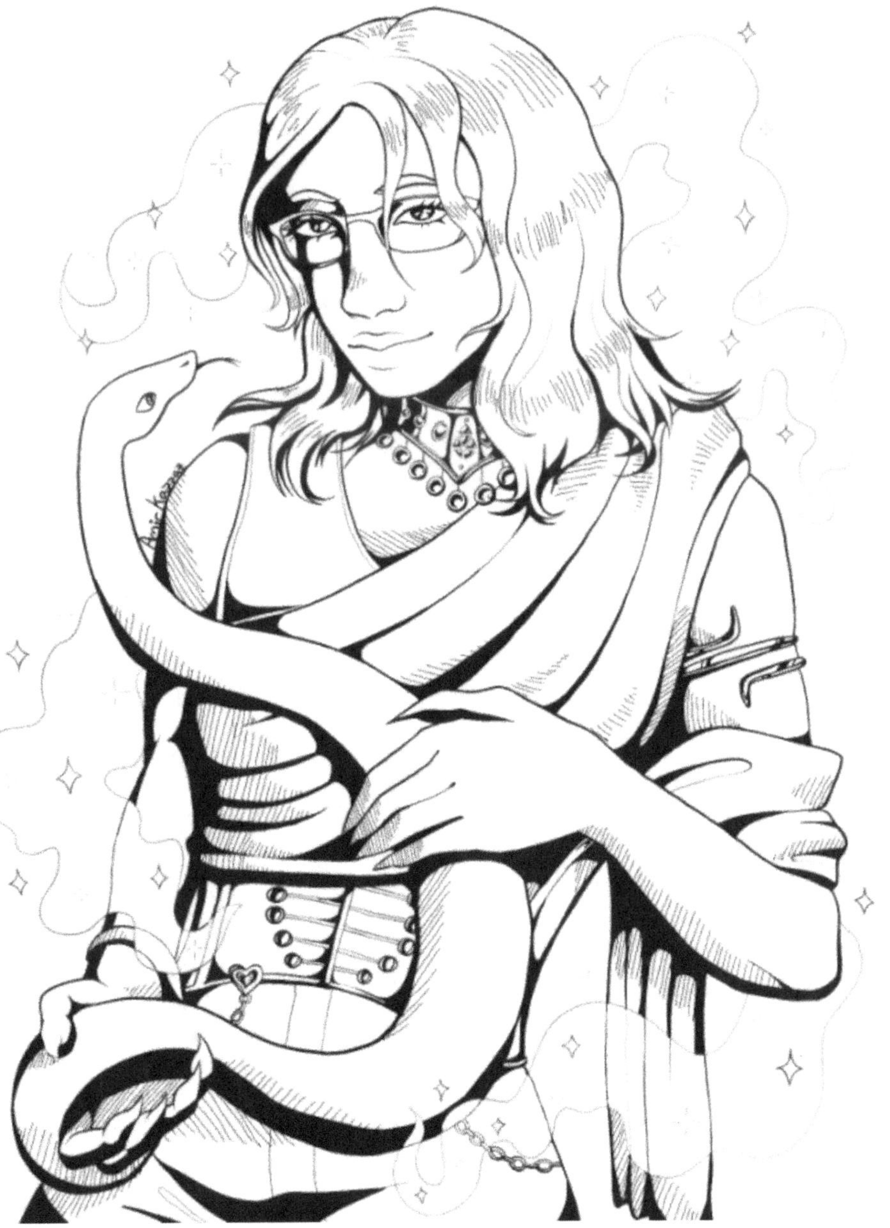

Don't let your fear get the best of you when you face the
terrifying beast in Operation Ground and Pound.

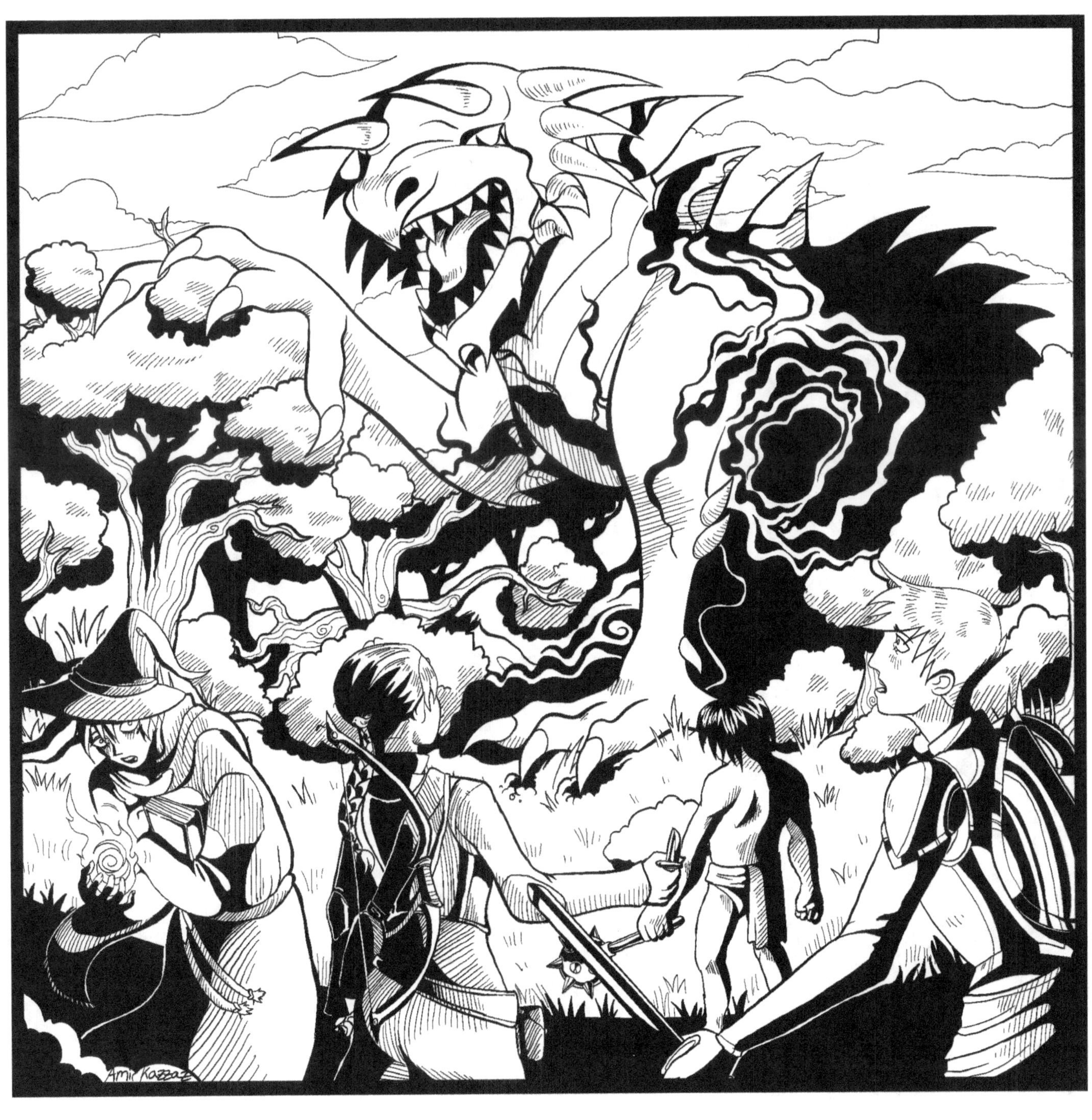

Beware the clutches of Lucious Clay's ghost when you try to steal his treasure!

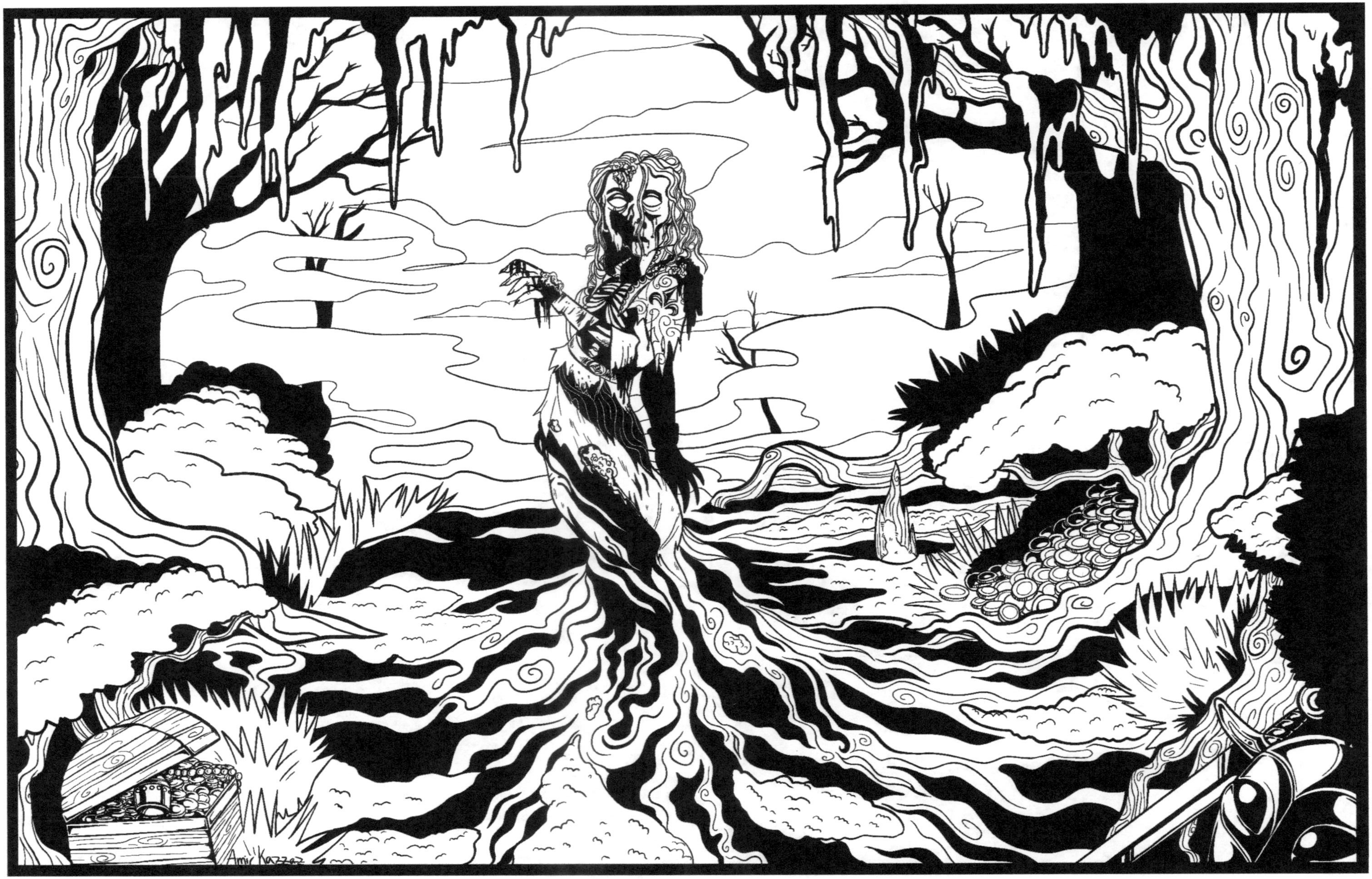

Don't follow this Trail of Tears too closely, unless you want to Nancy Drew some clues as to what happened to these people in Aftermath.

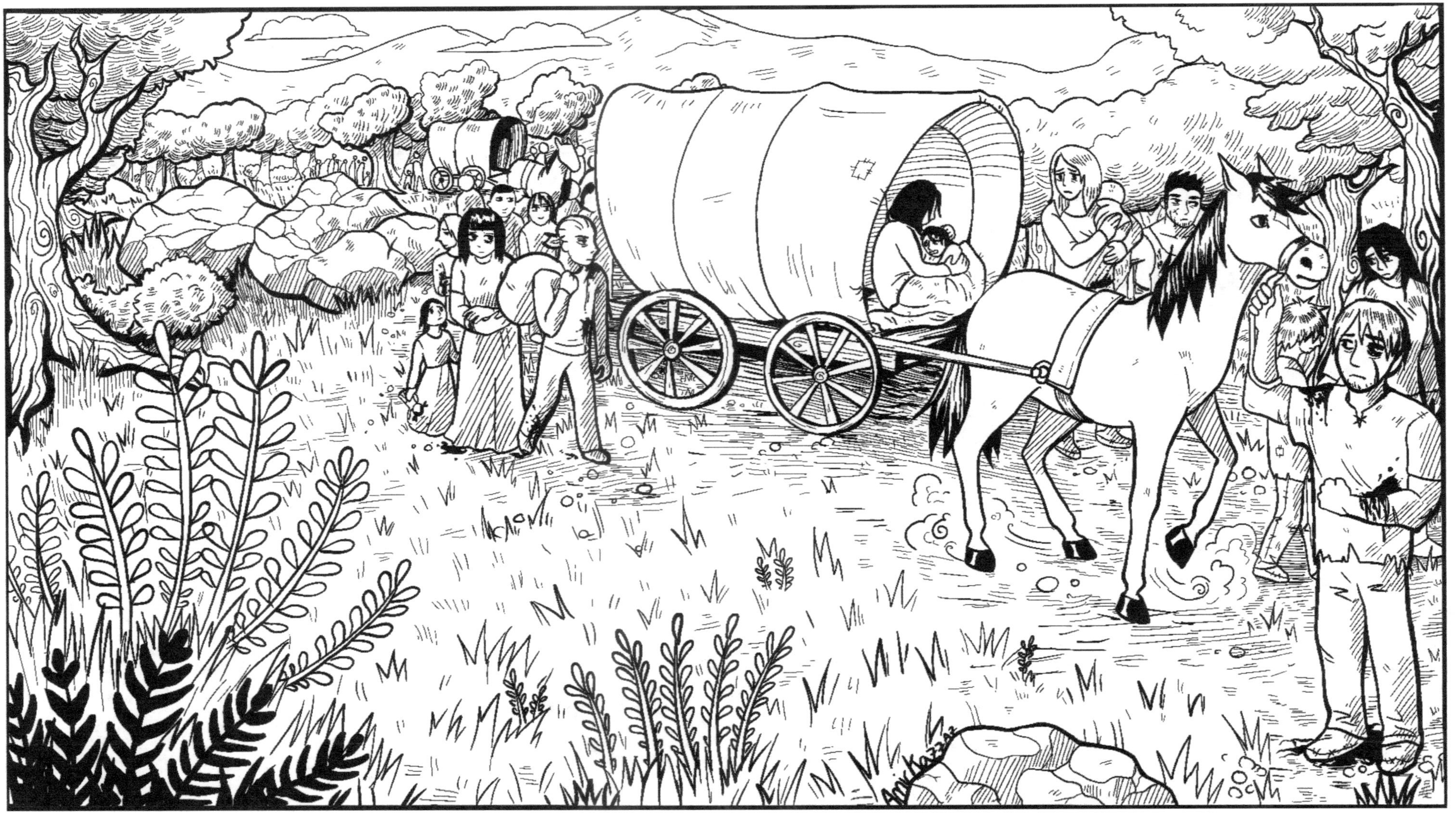

Not everything has to be about steel weapons and sorcery. Sometimes it's best to go with an Alternative Attack Action. How about a knuckle sandwich, perhaps?

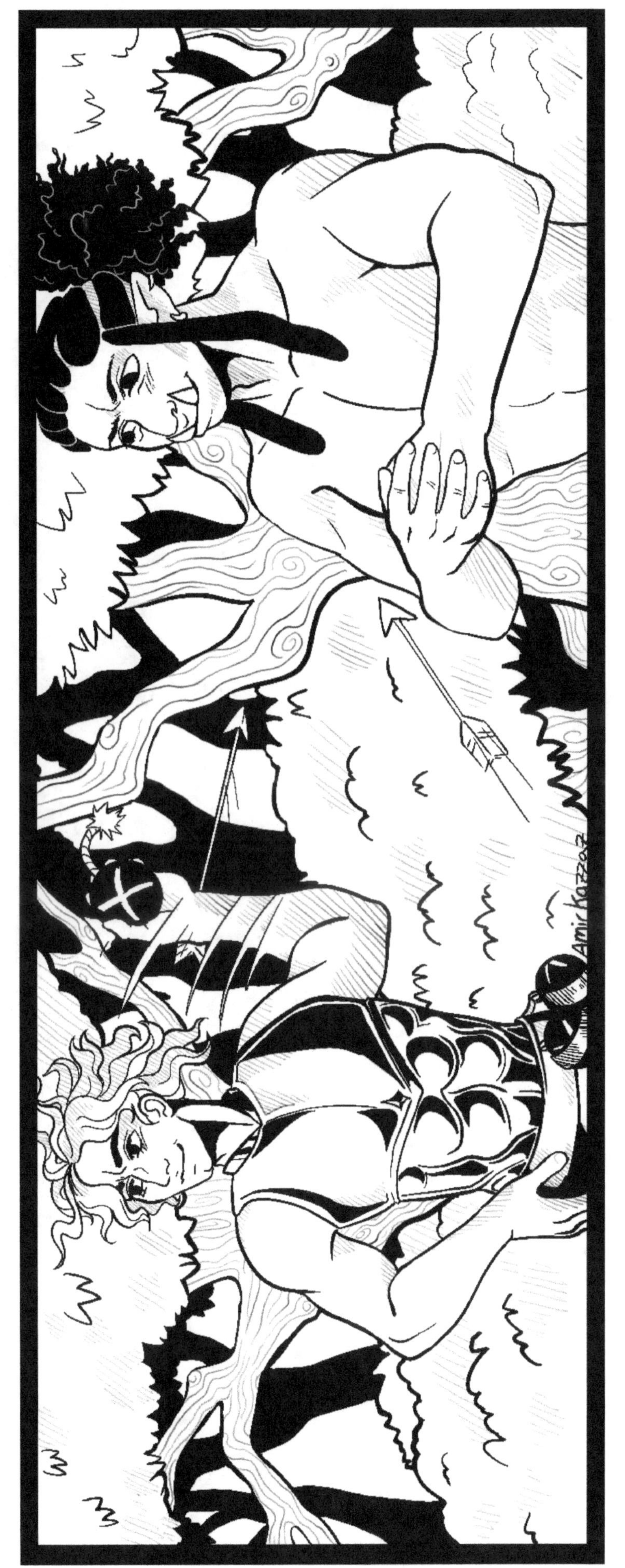

After a long day on the mission, it's time for the party to make camp for the night.

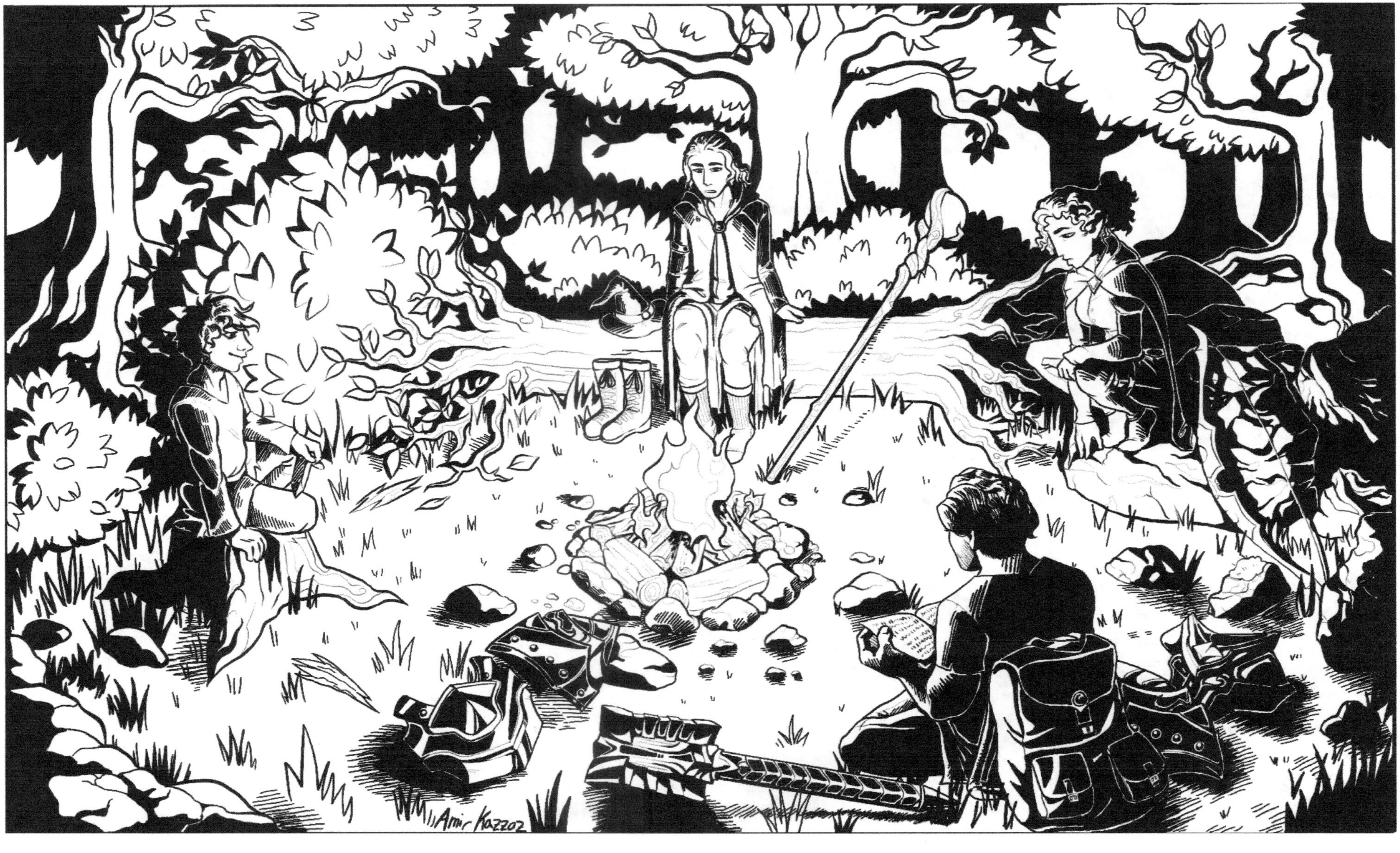

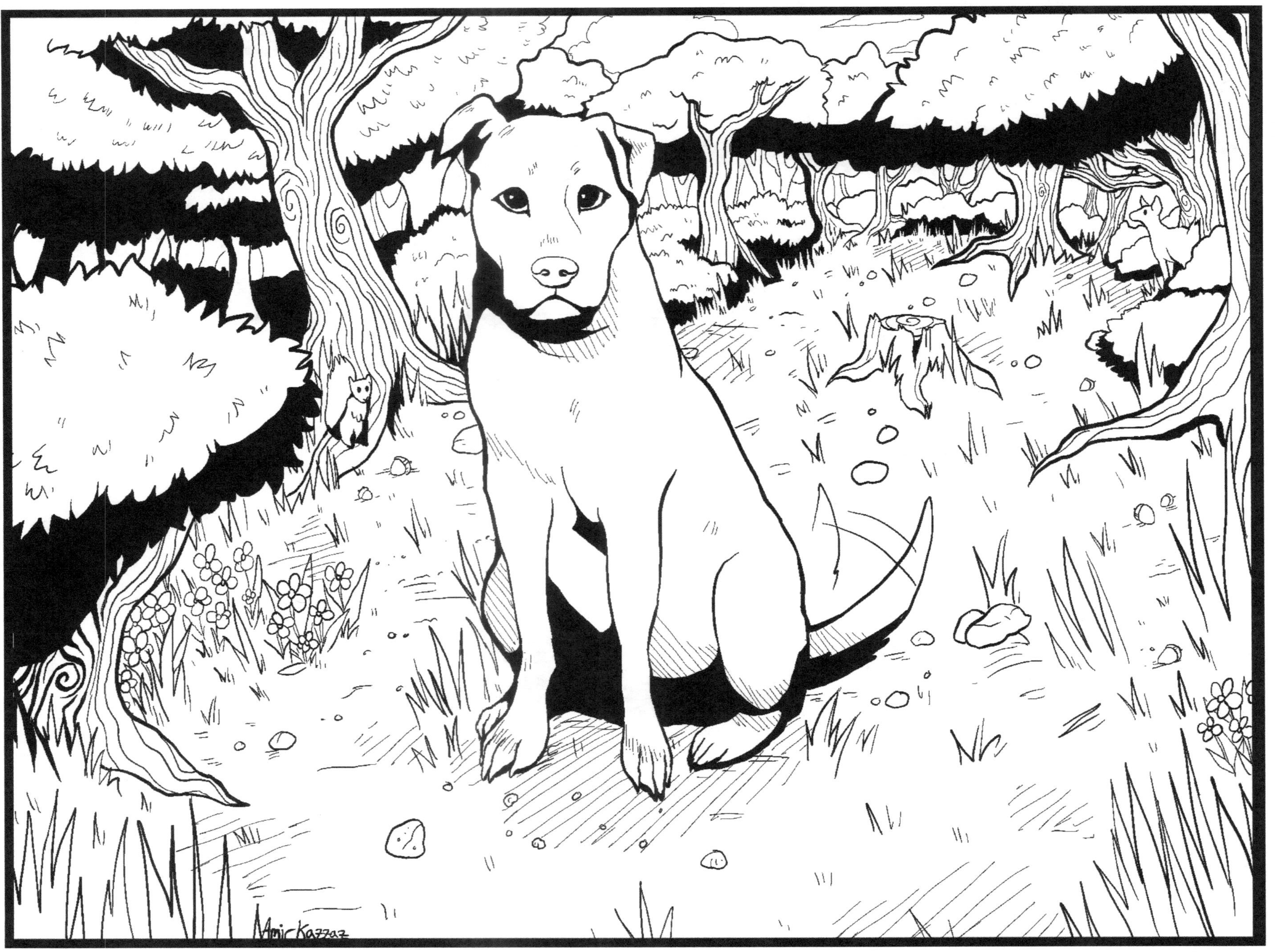

Now THAT is a good boy!

Don't be too surprised if an Arcanite pops out from strange places, like in Oh, Mummy. You never know what kind of shenanigans they are up to.

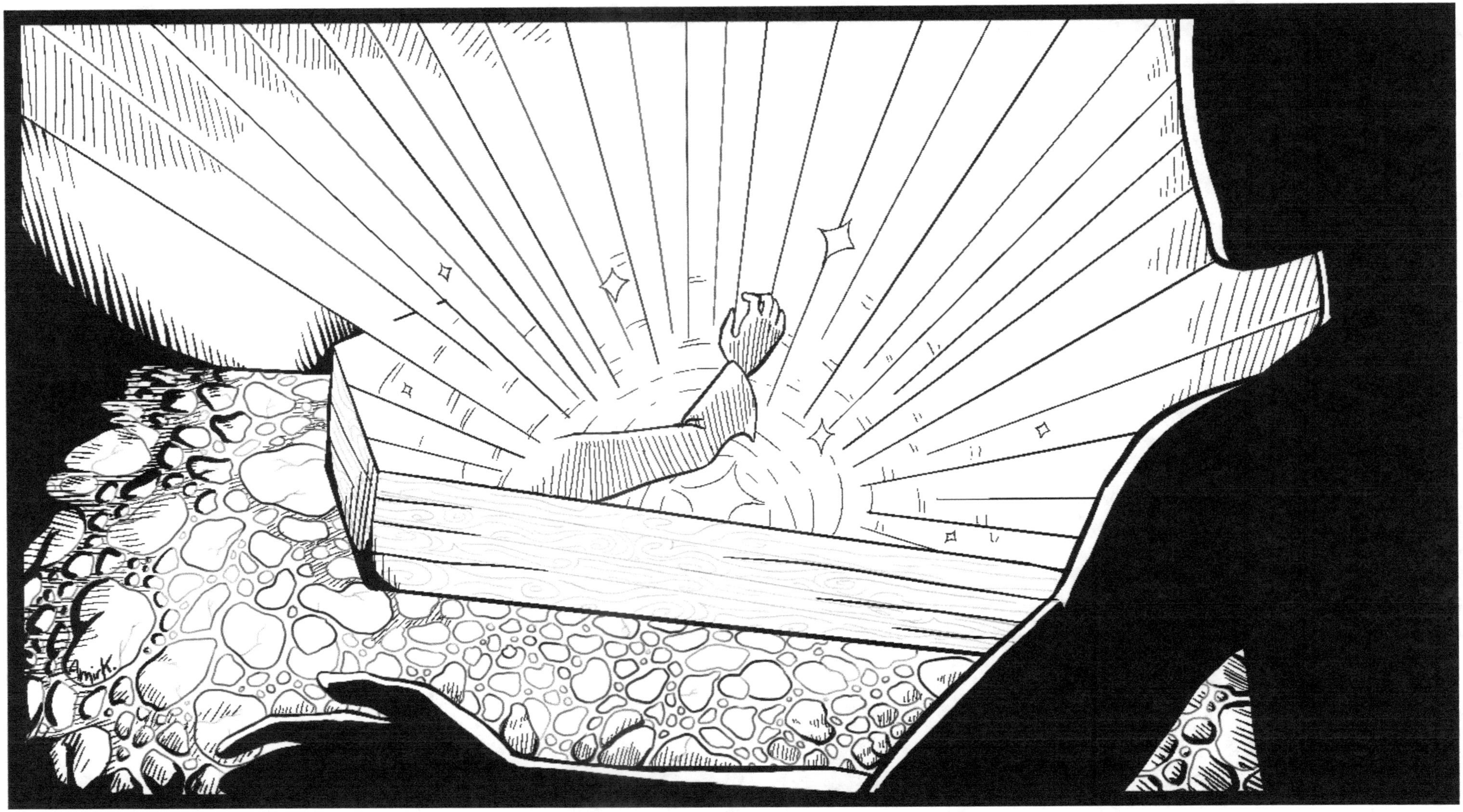

What evil could this retched fiend have planned? You may just find out if you play The Fugees.

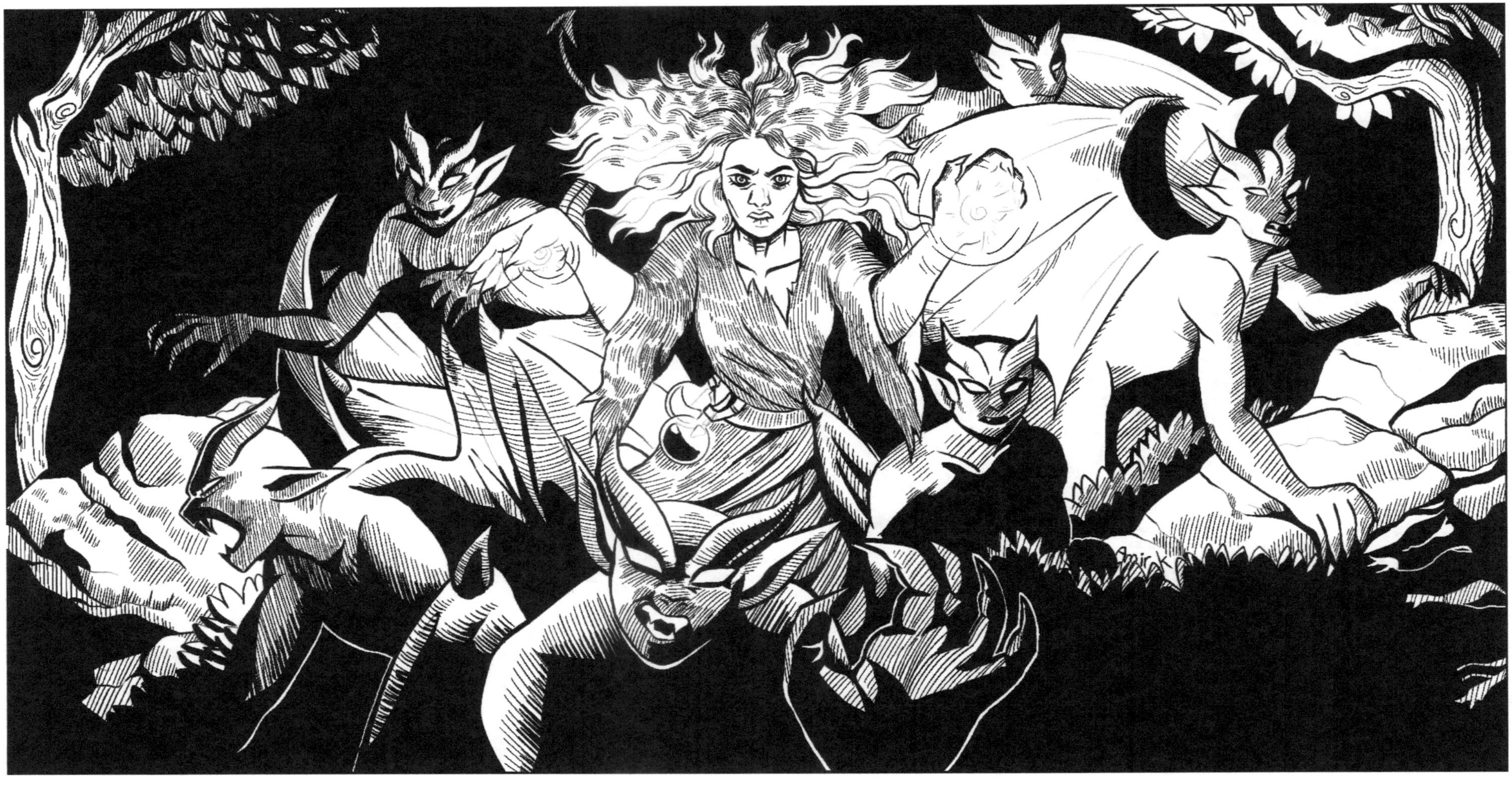

Why risk losing all of your stuff while you're out in the field. There's no better or safer place to store your things than The Storehouse. You will hardly ever get robbed or have your consumables ravaged by swarms of rats.

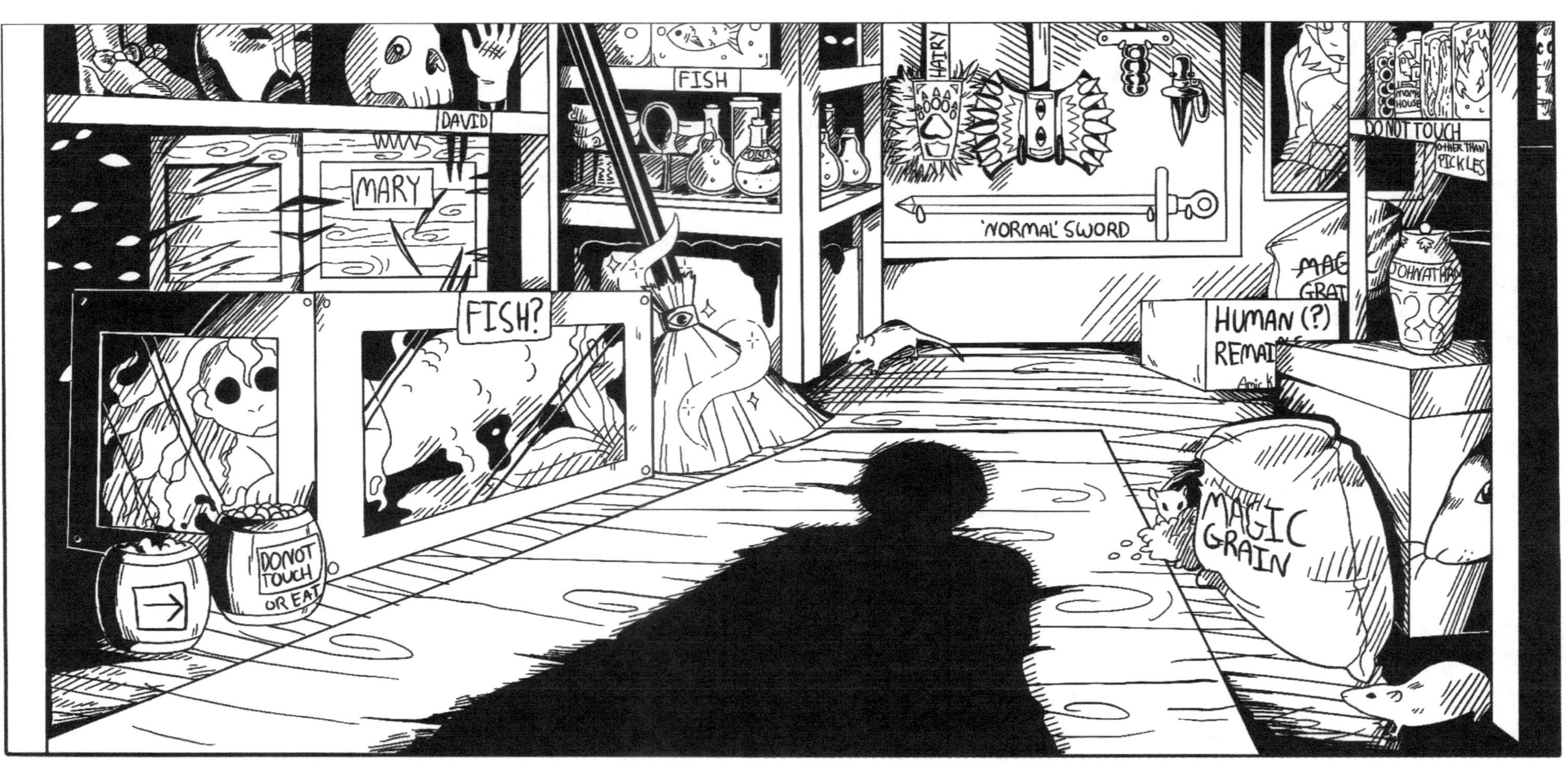

ANTHONY

Anthony Alvarado is an artist based out of San Antonio, Texas. After graduating from college, he began working toward realizing a career as a full time freelance concept artist. His focus has been on traditional acrylic painting, charcoal, graphite and, more recently, digital painting. You can check out his ever-growing portfolio on Instagram: @artbytony.

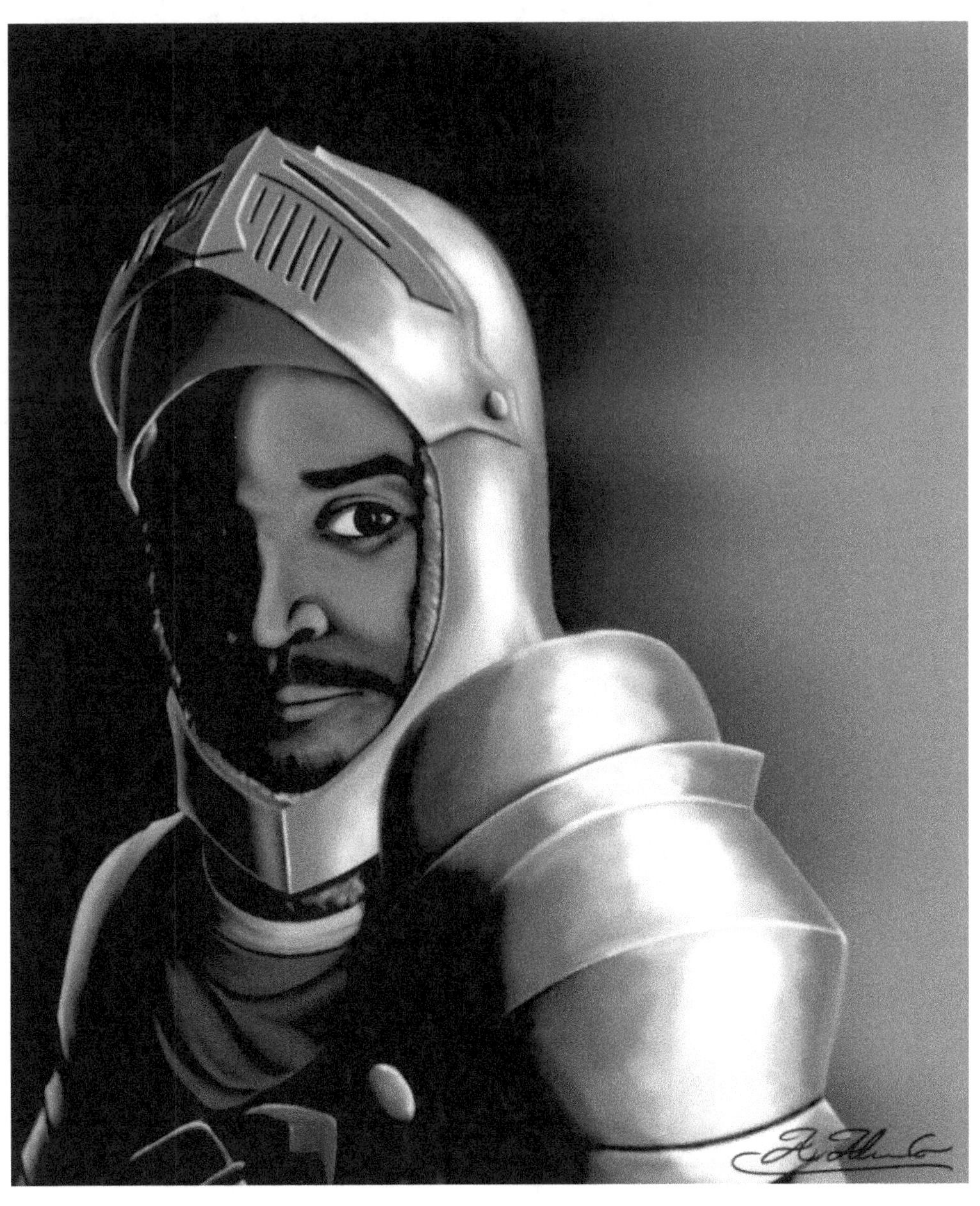

You never know what monsters you will encounter in The Consortium.

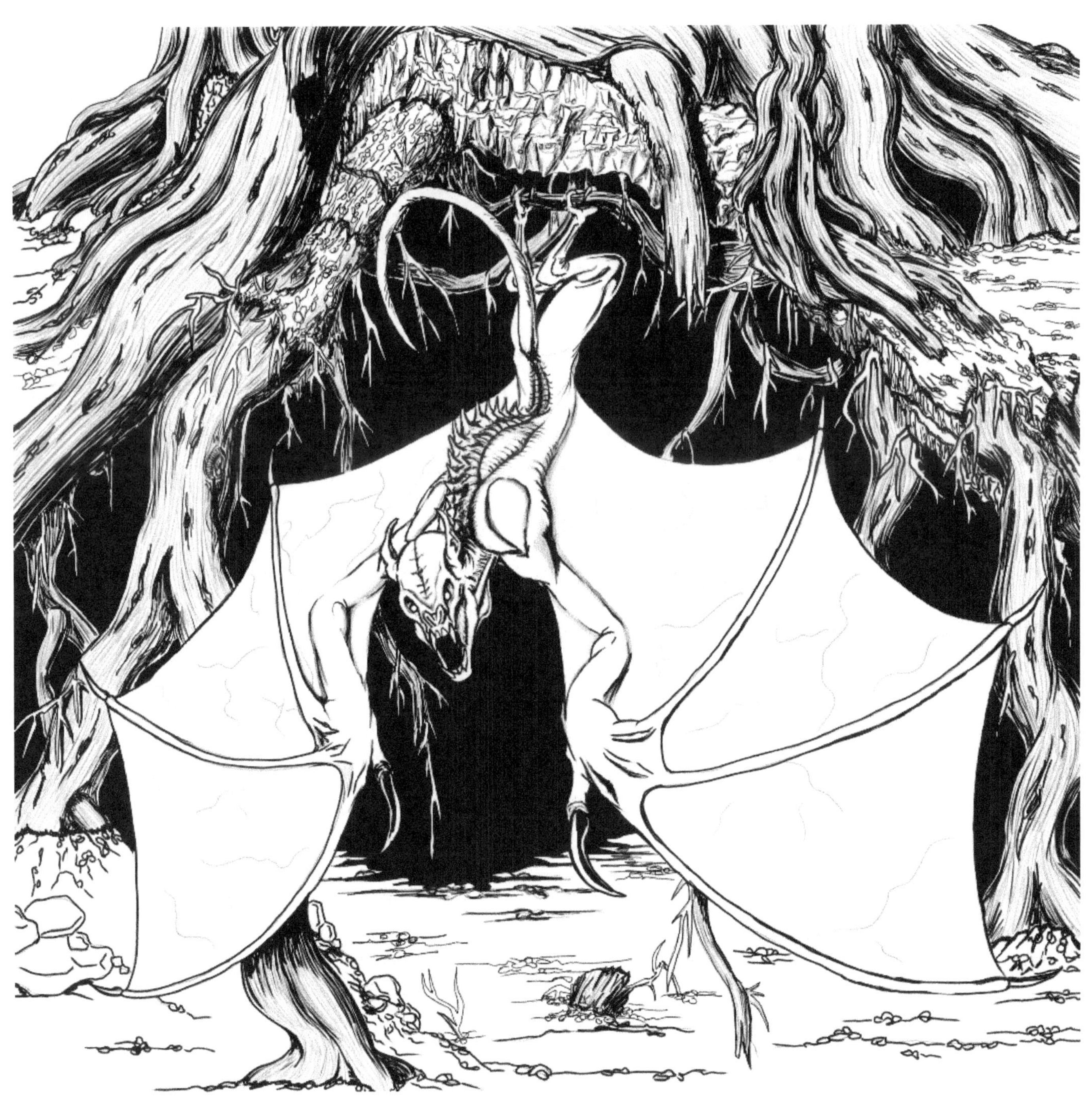

Lurking in the shadows, waiting for their chance to attack.

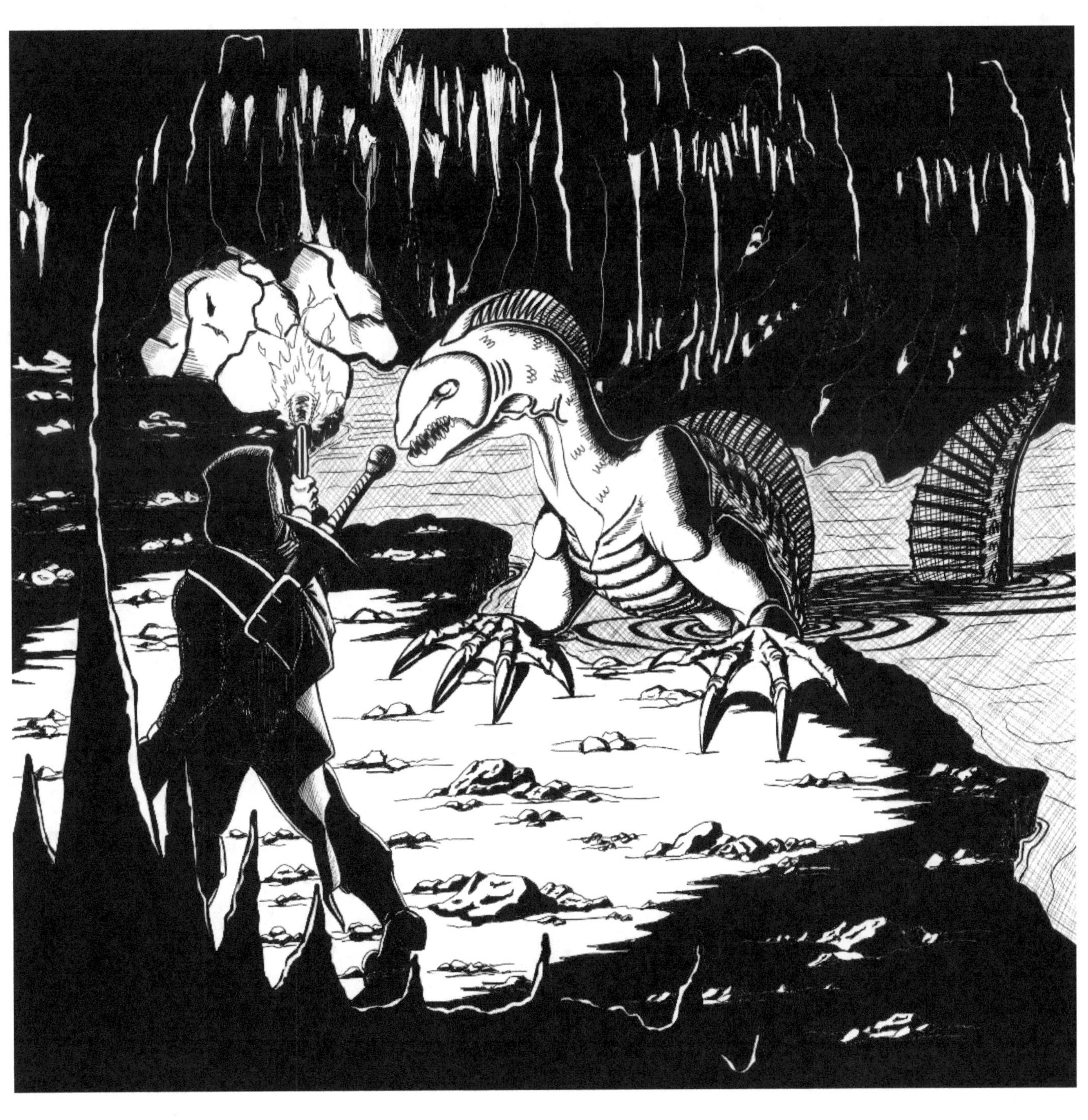

So keep your Hirelngs close, and your Brothers in Arms closer!

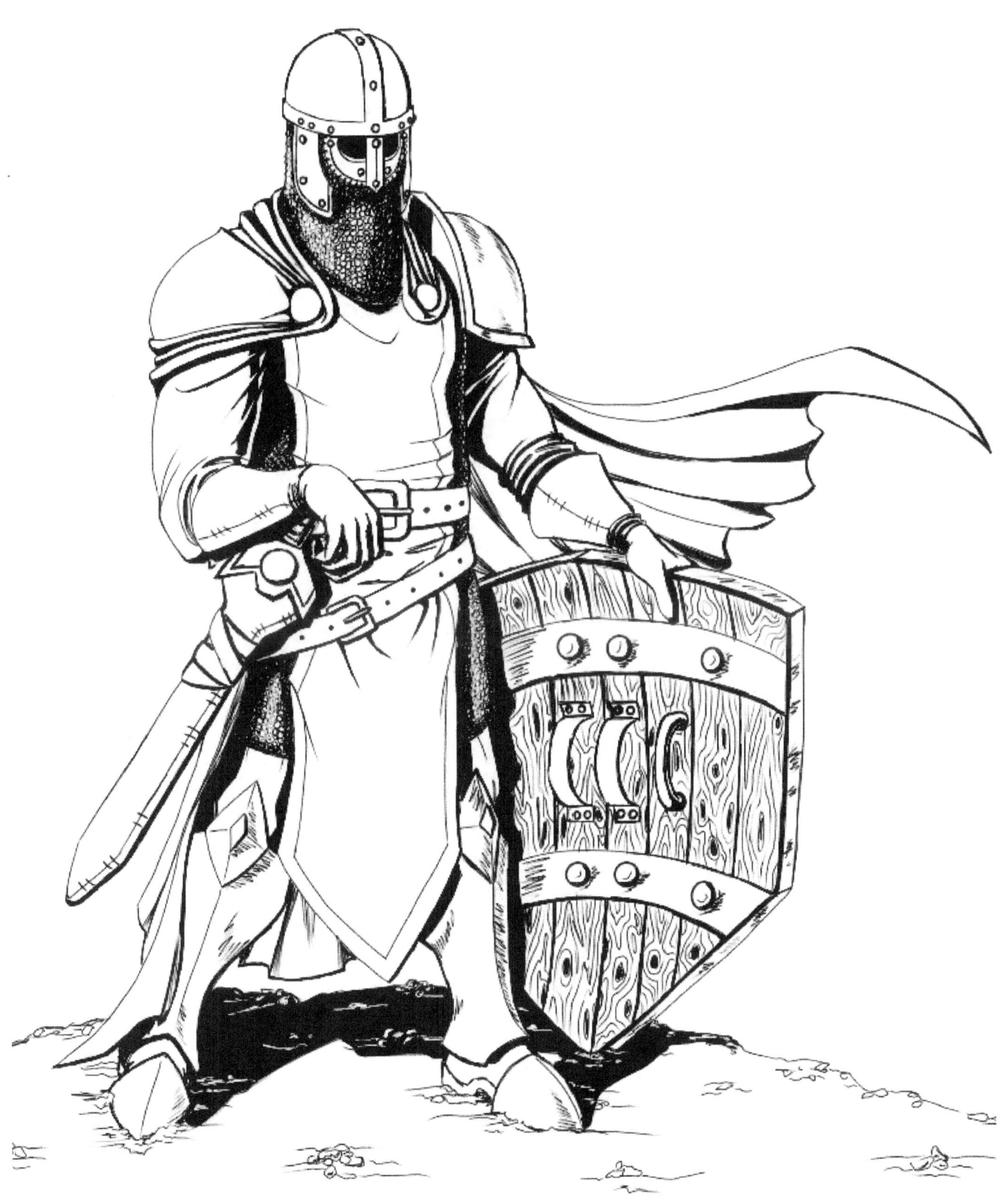

A little Power Bolt never killed anybody… Well, except maybe that guy.

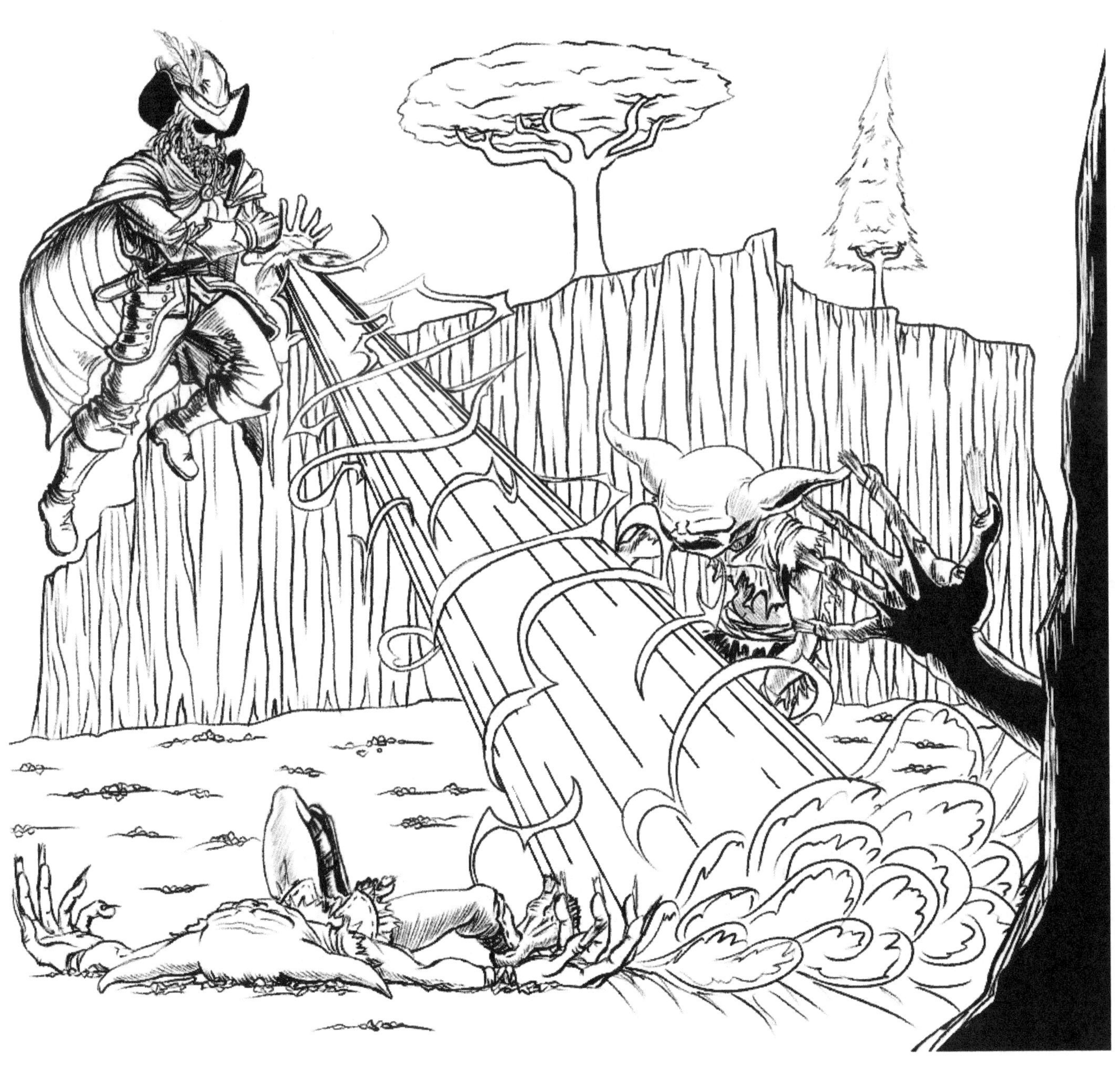

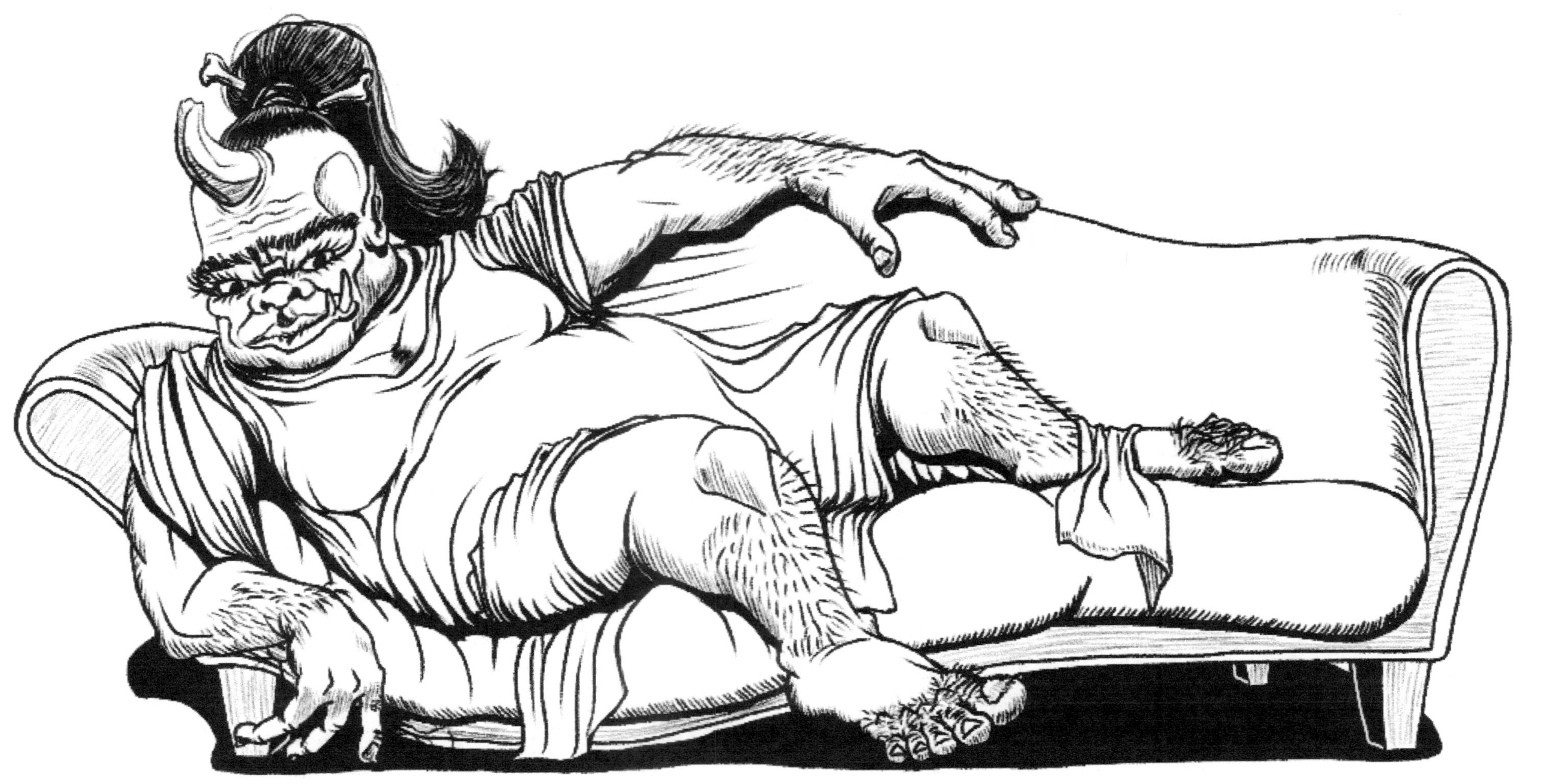

Paint me like one of your Elf Girls!

Always stand your ground when faced with even the most impossible situations. Besides, what's so bad about rolling on the Serious Injuries List, anyway?

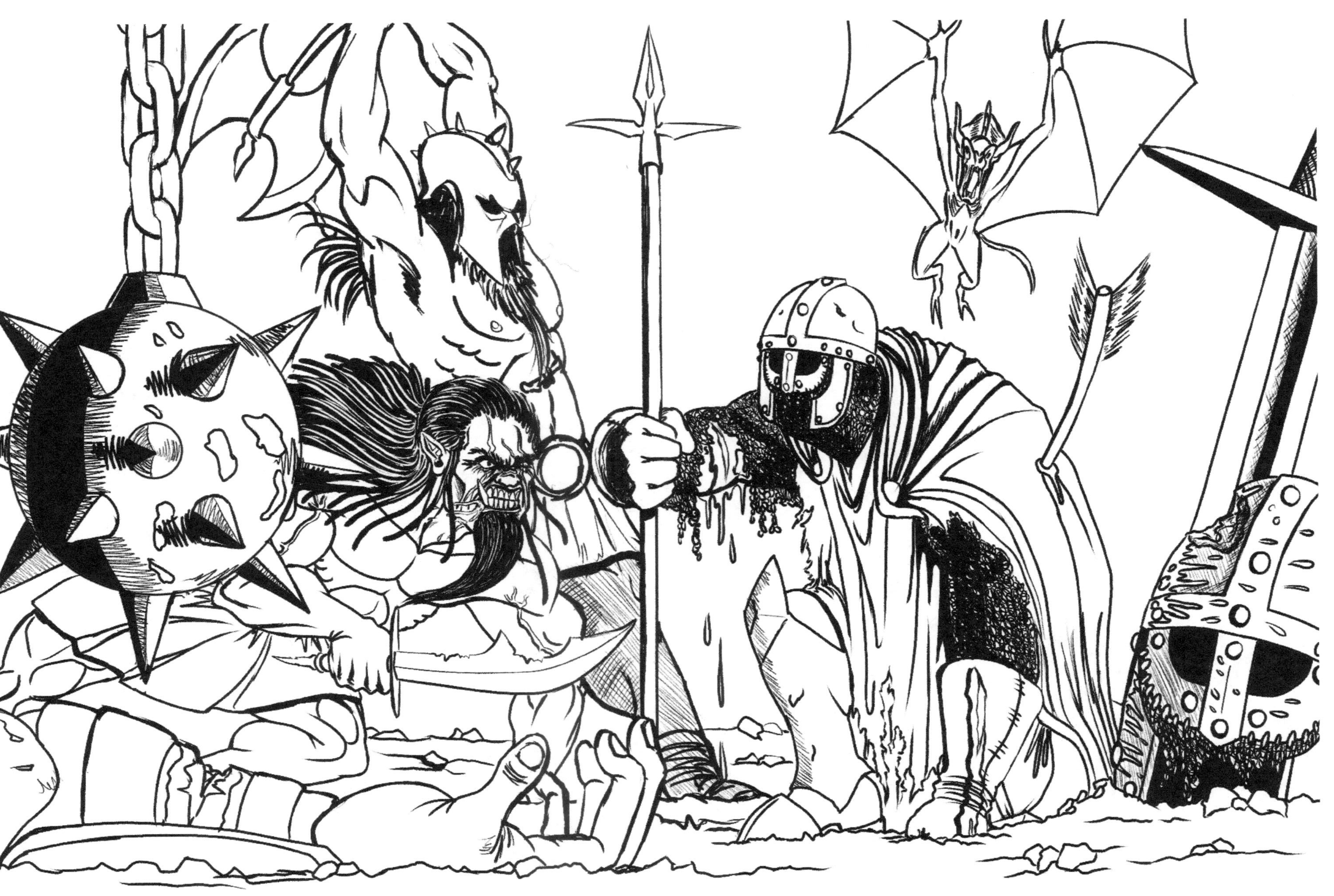

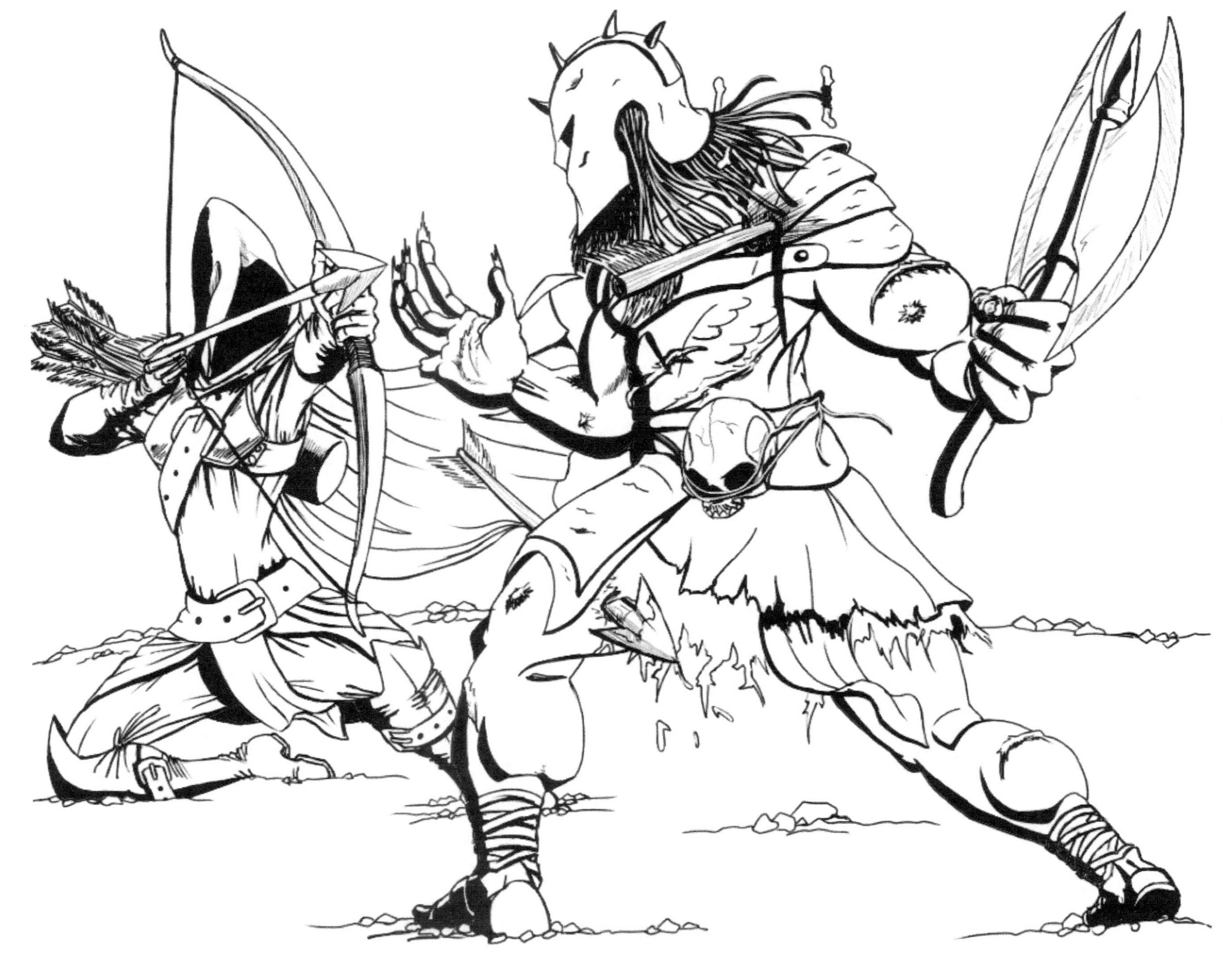

A little Guild Training could go a long way to ready you for the trials ahead.

Beware the foreboding altar…

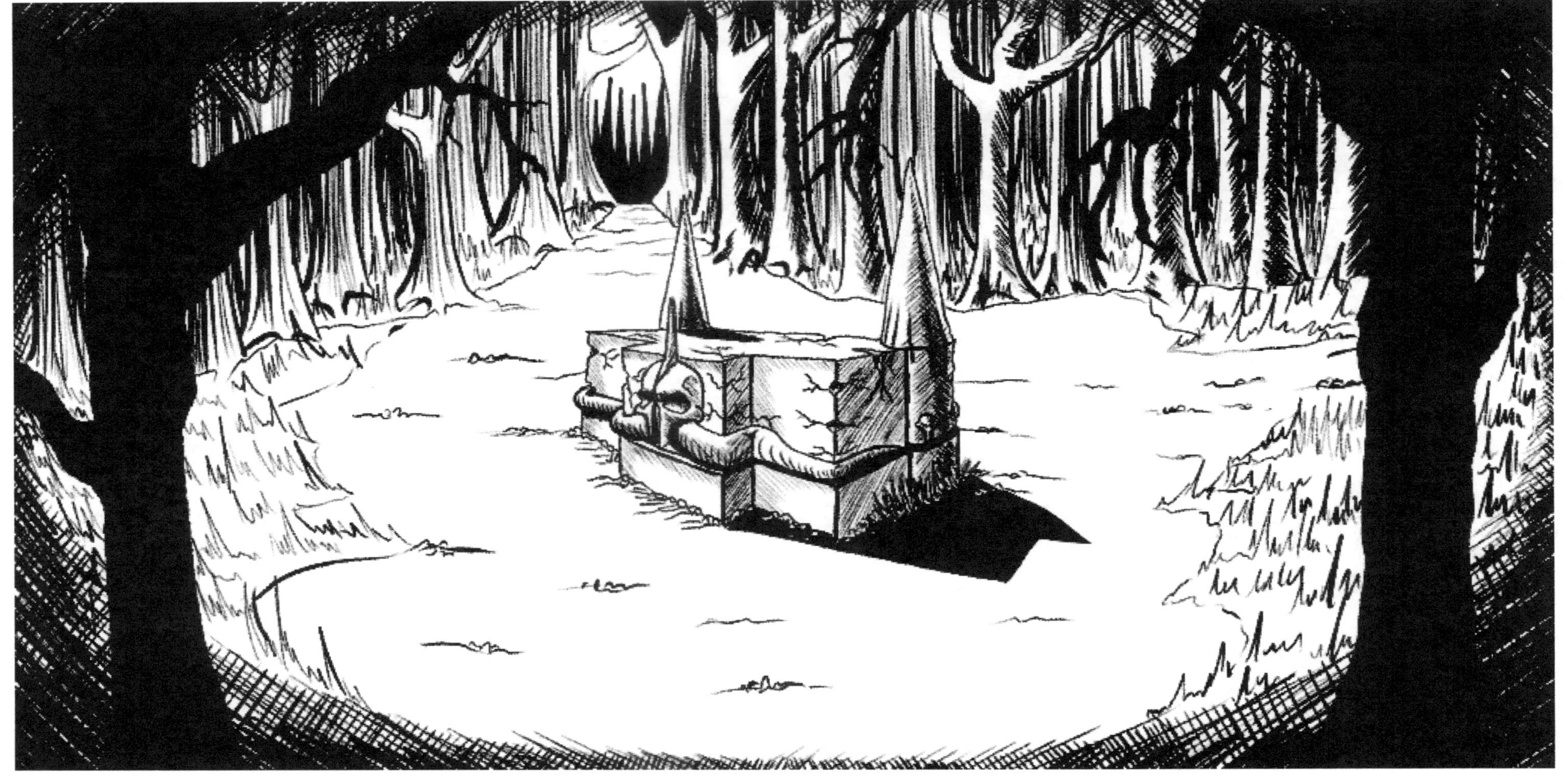

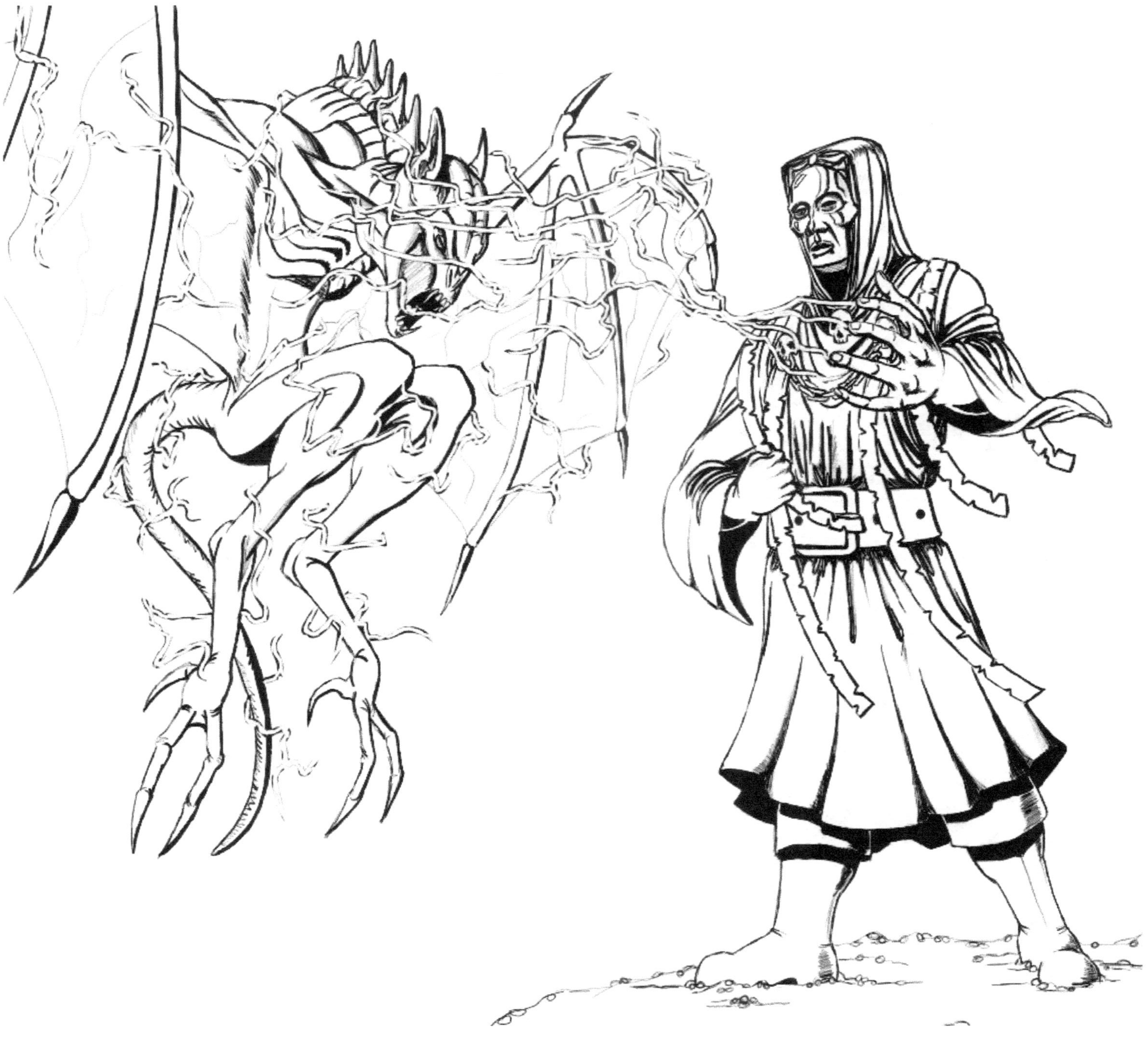

A Bound
monster is the
best kind of
monster, I
always say.

BLAIR

Blair Vaessen is an artist living in the greater Chicagoland area. Her love of art has led her down the path of freelancing. Her work is inspired by anime/manga, cartoons and fantasy ttrpgs. When not being held captive at her retail job, she can be found drawing or gaming. You can check out her portfolio at bevaessen.wixsite.com/blairart and get in contact with her at bevaessen@gmail.com.

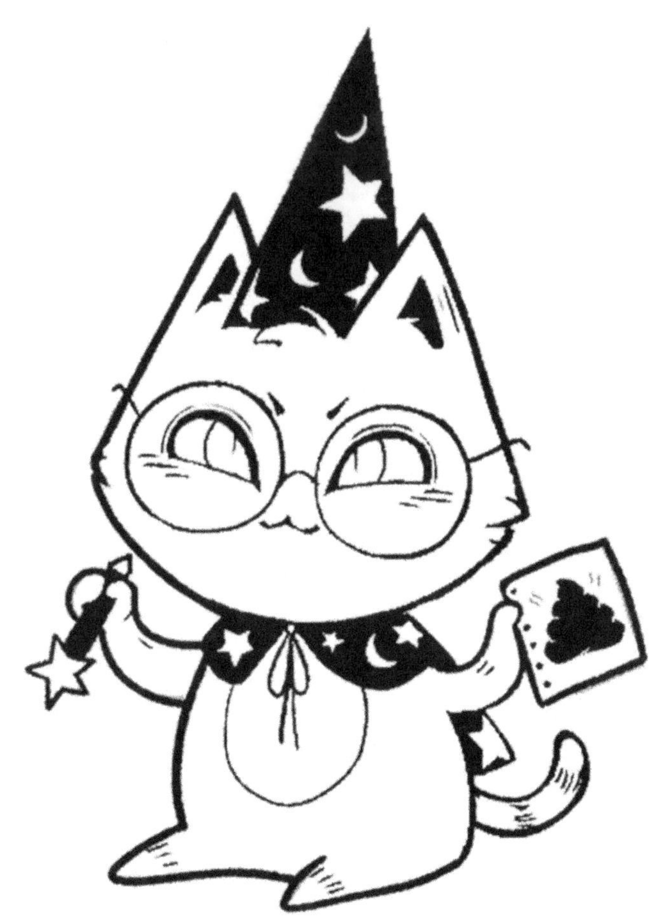

If you see some monks starving themselves for a cause,
you may end up getting roped into A Quiet Riot.

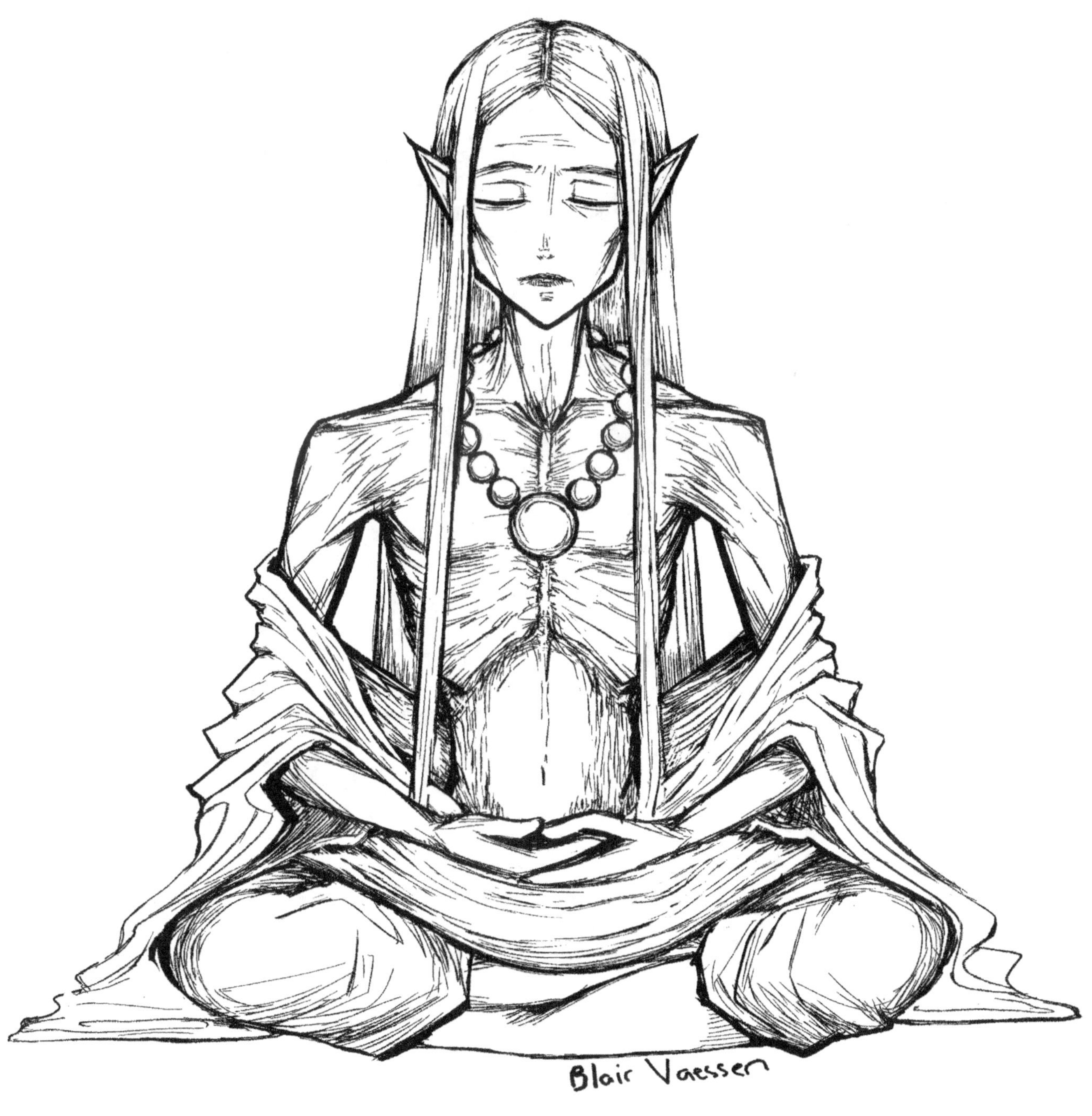

If you were epic enough to collect all of the Legendary
Artifacts, you wouldn't care how you look, either!

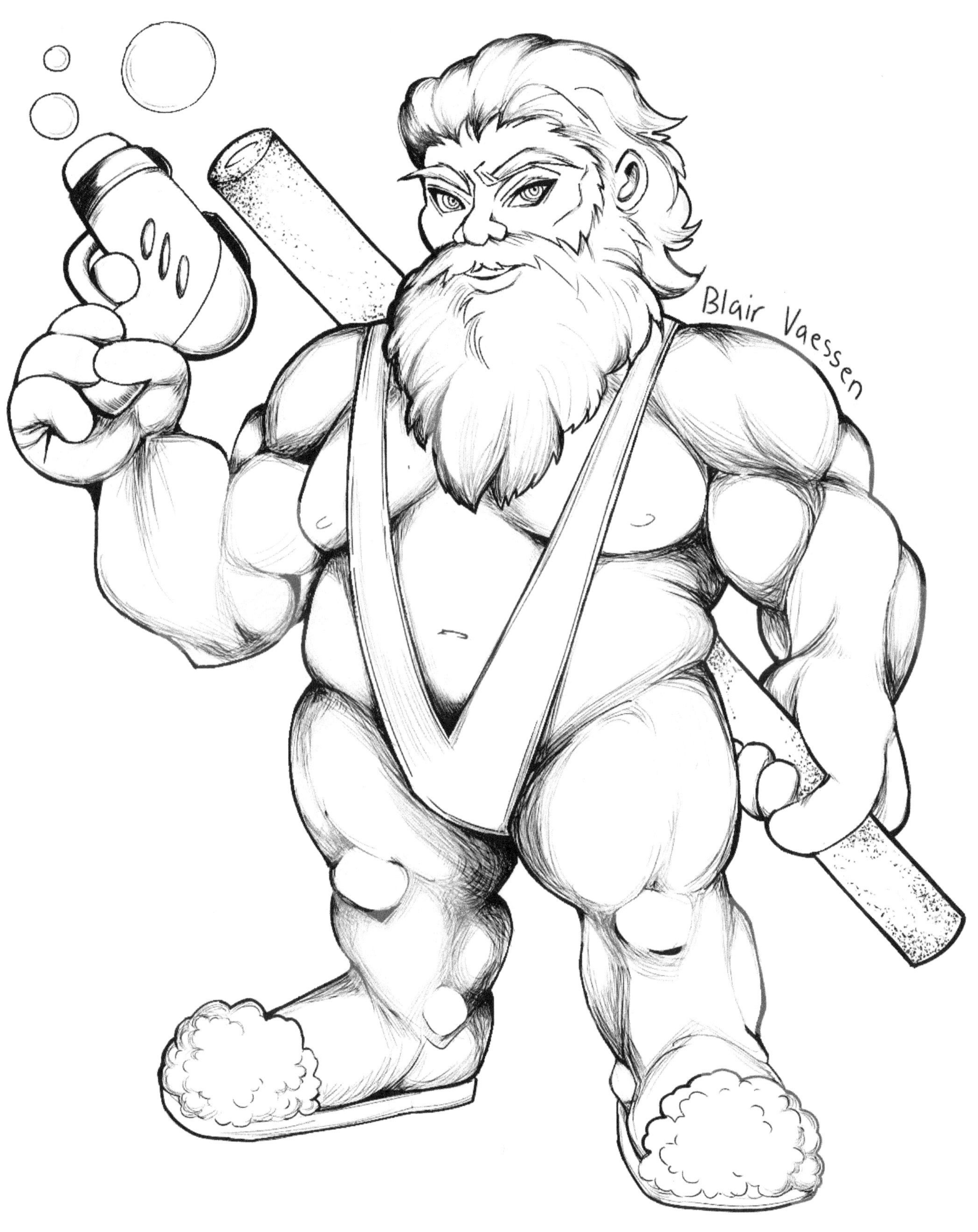

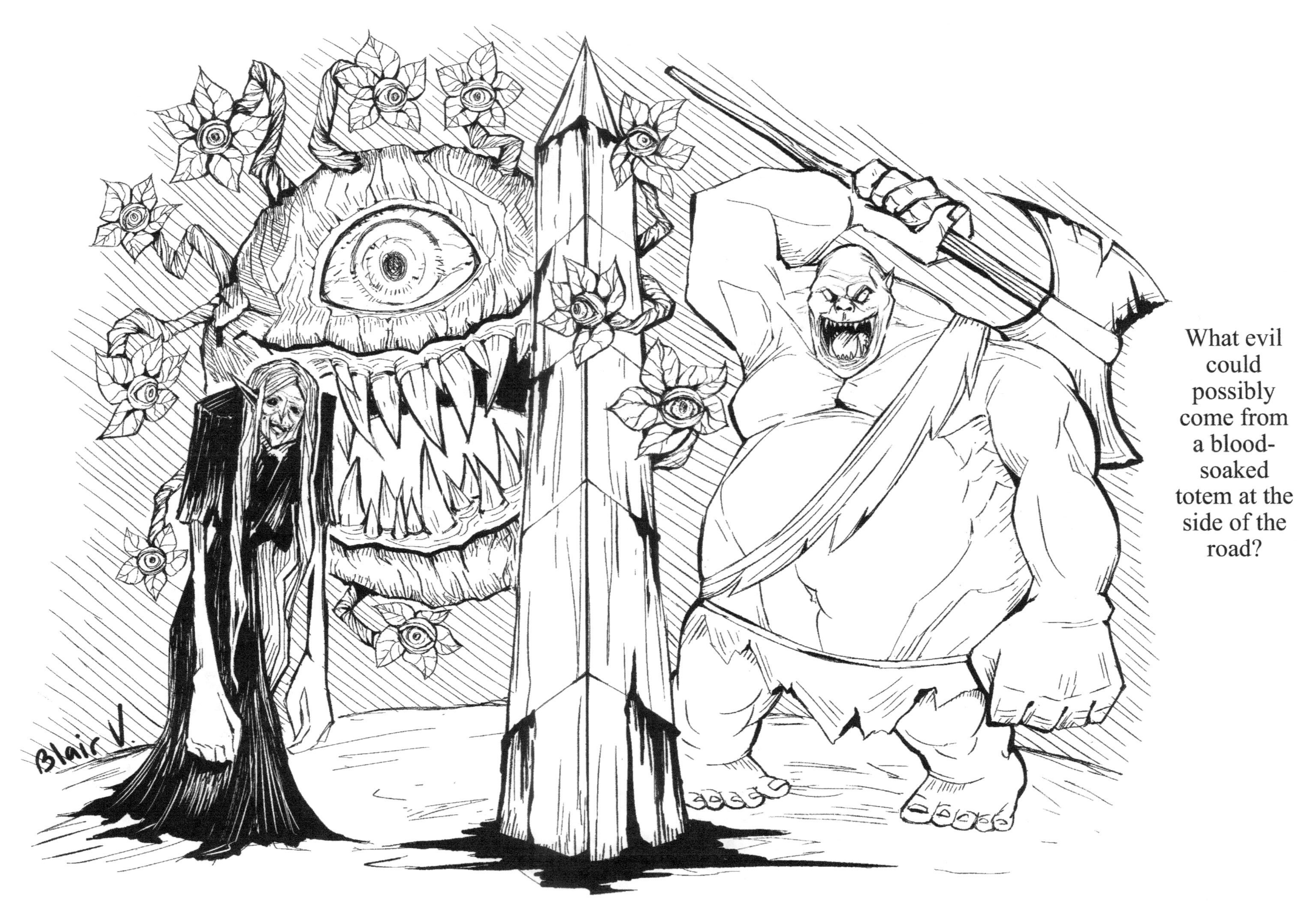

What evil could possibly come from a blood-soaked totem at the side of the road?

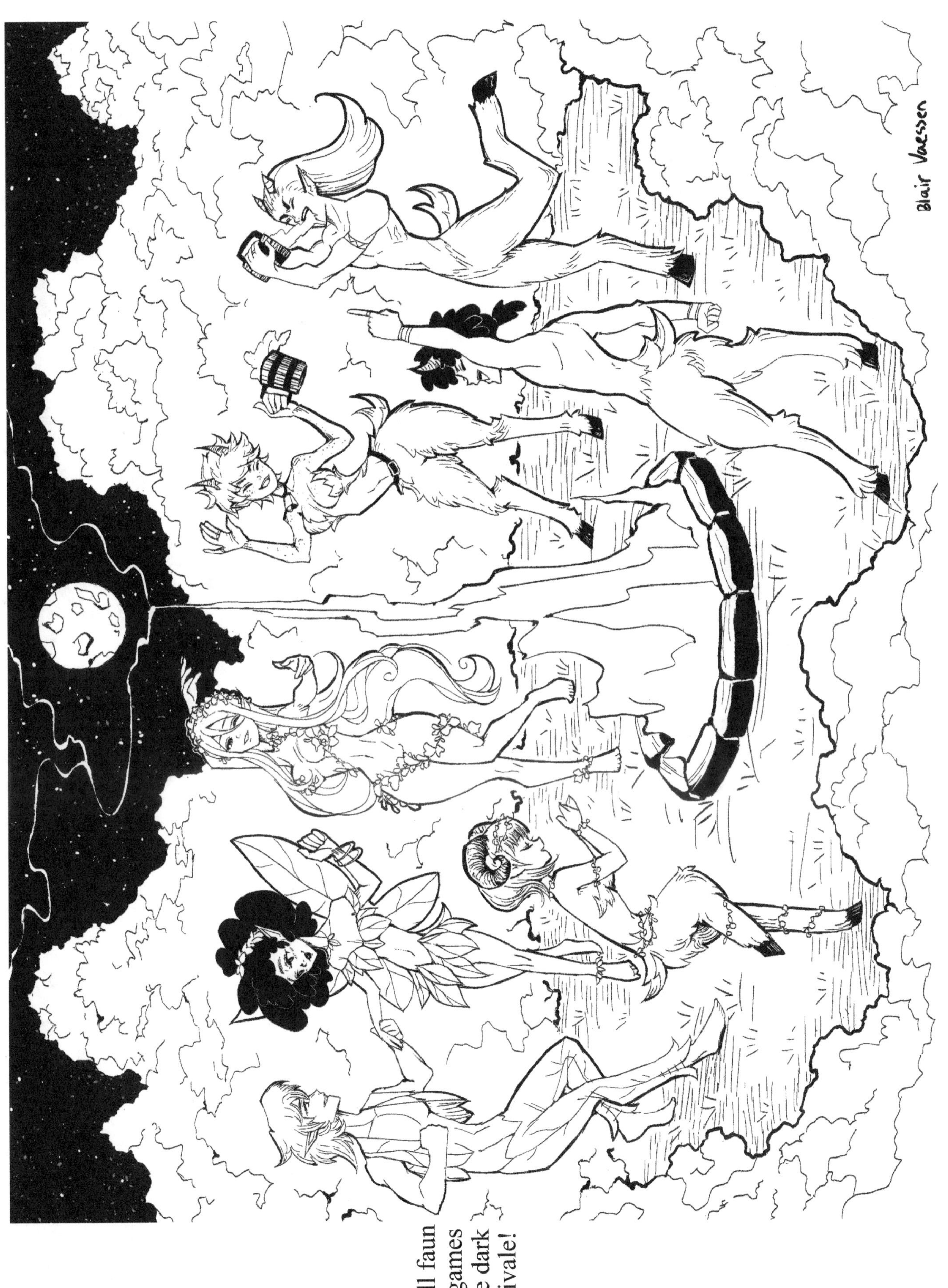

It's all faun and games at the dark carnivale!

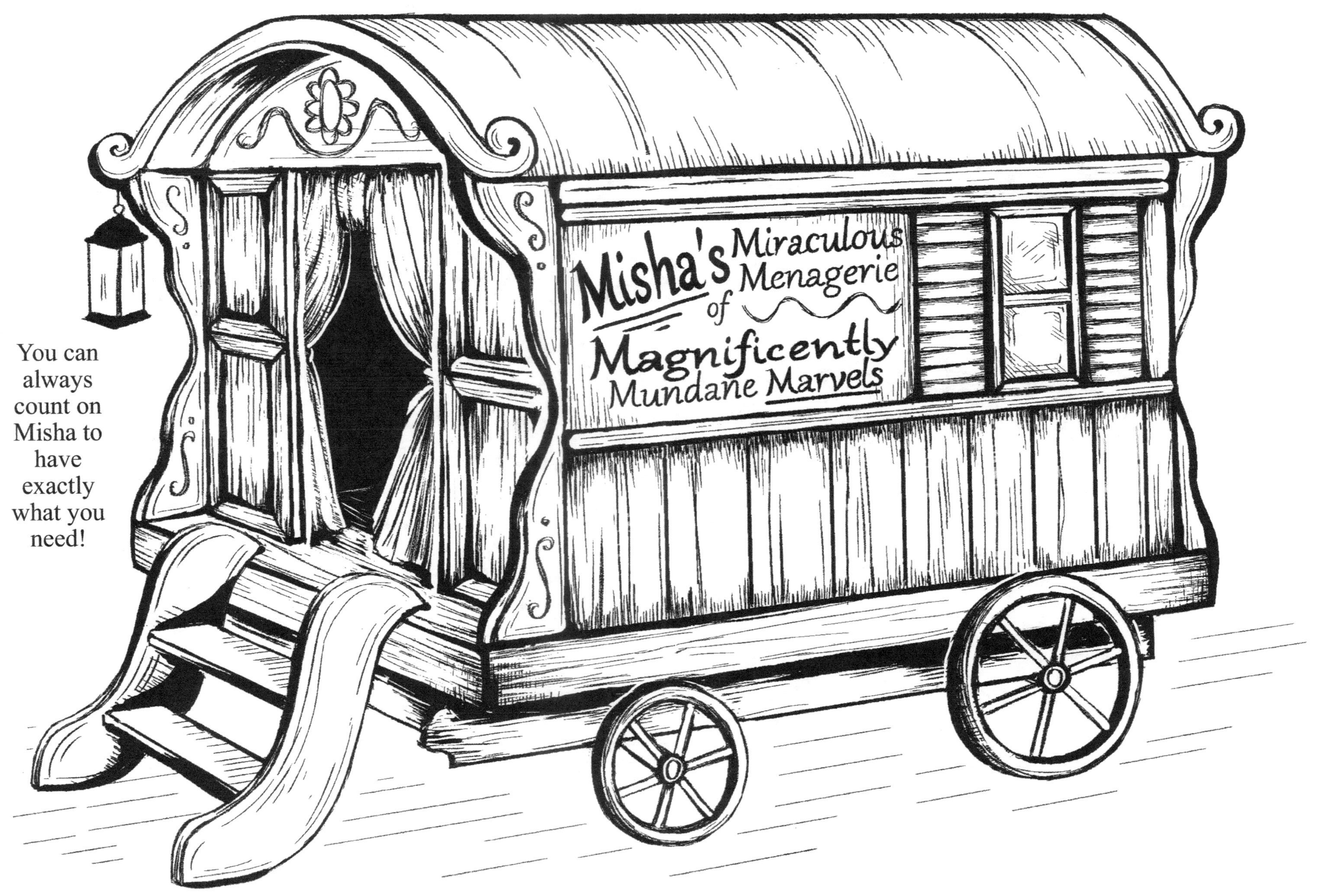

Misha's Miraculous Menagerie
of
Magnificently Mundane Marvels
You can always count on Misha to have exactly what you need!

Guess it's time to make a new character! What will you play next?

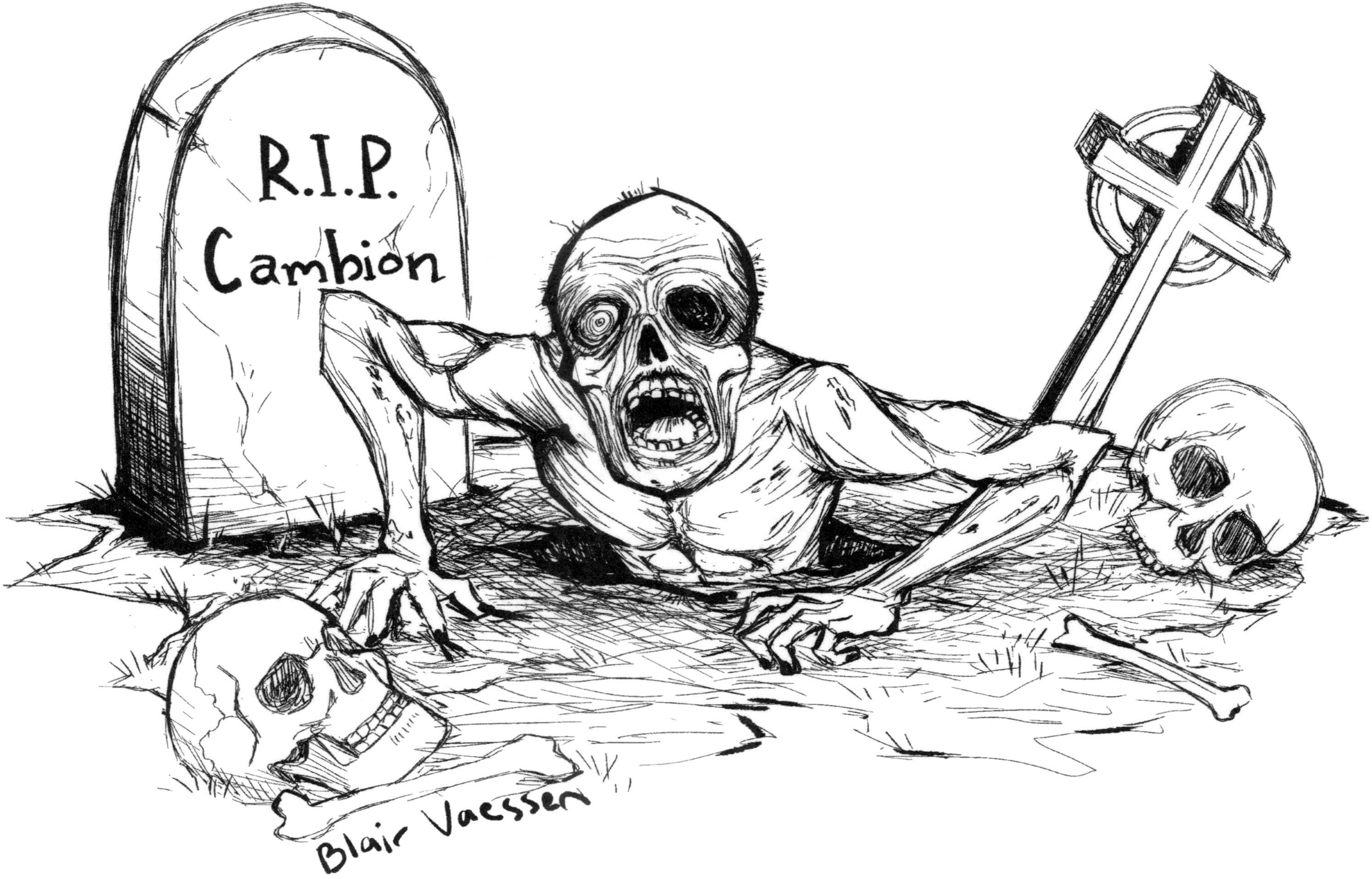

Have some extra Guilder and a little moxie? Seek
out the Runesmith on Fascination Street to give
your equipment a little more bang for your buck.

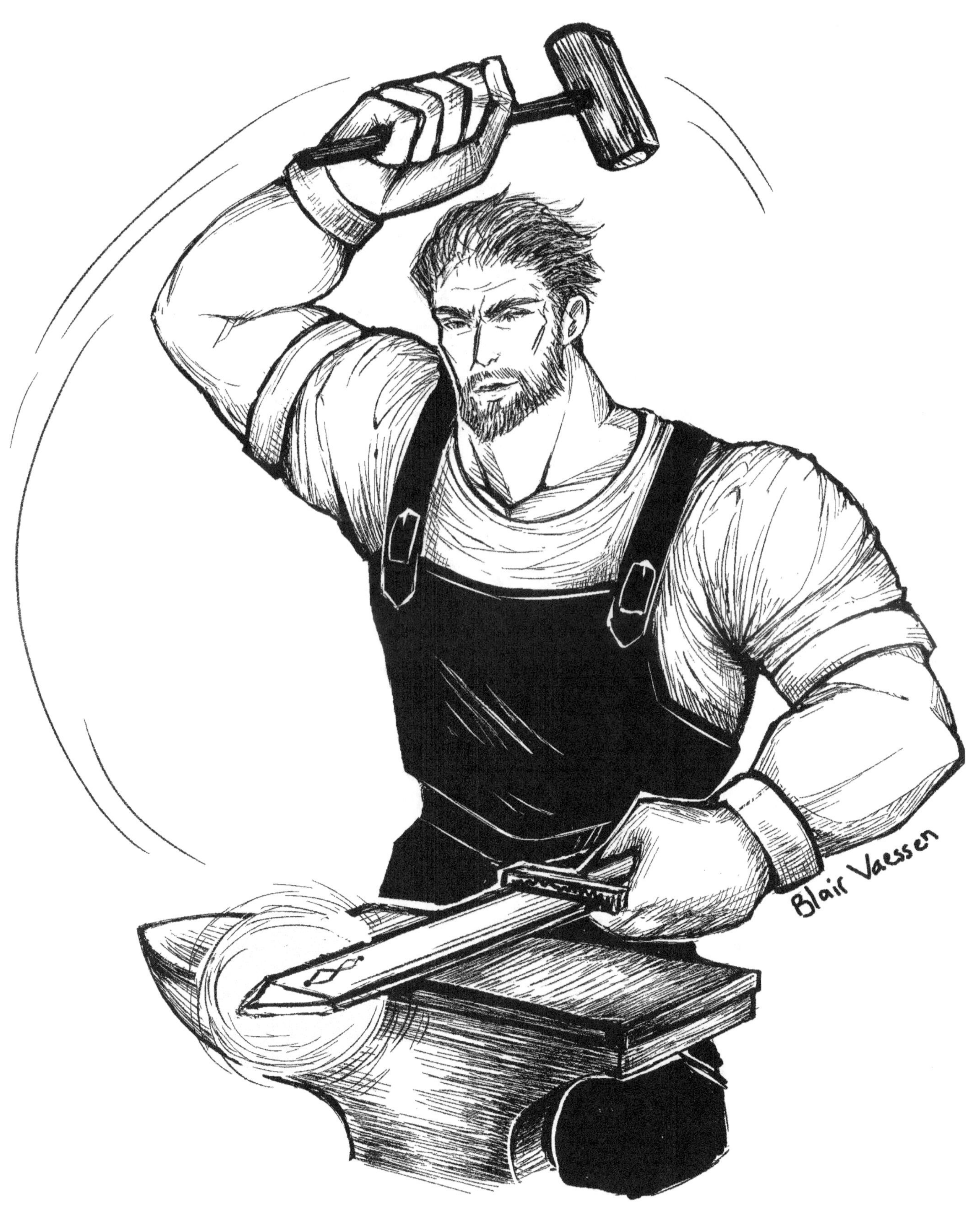

Those little street urchins sure know how to hustle.
Watch out for this one, he's hard to get rid of.

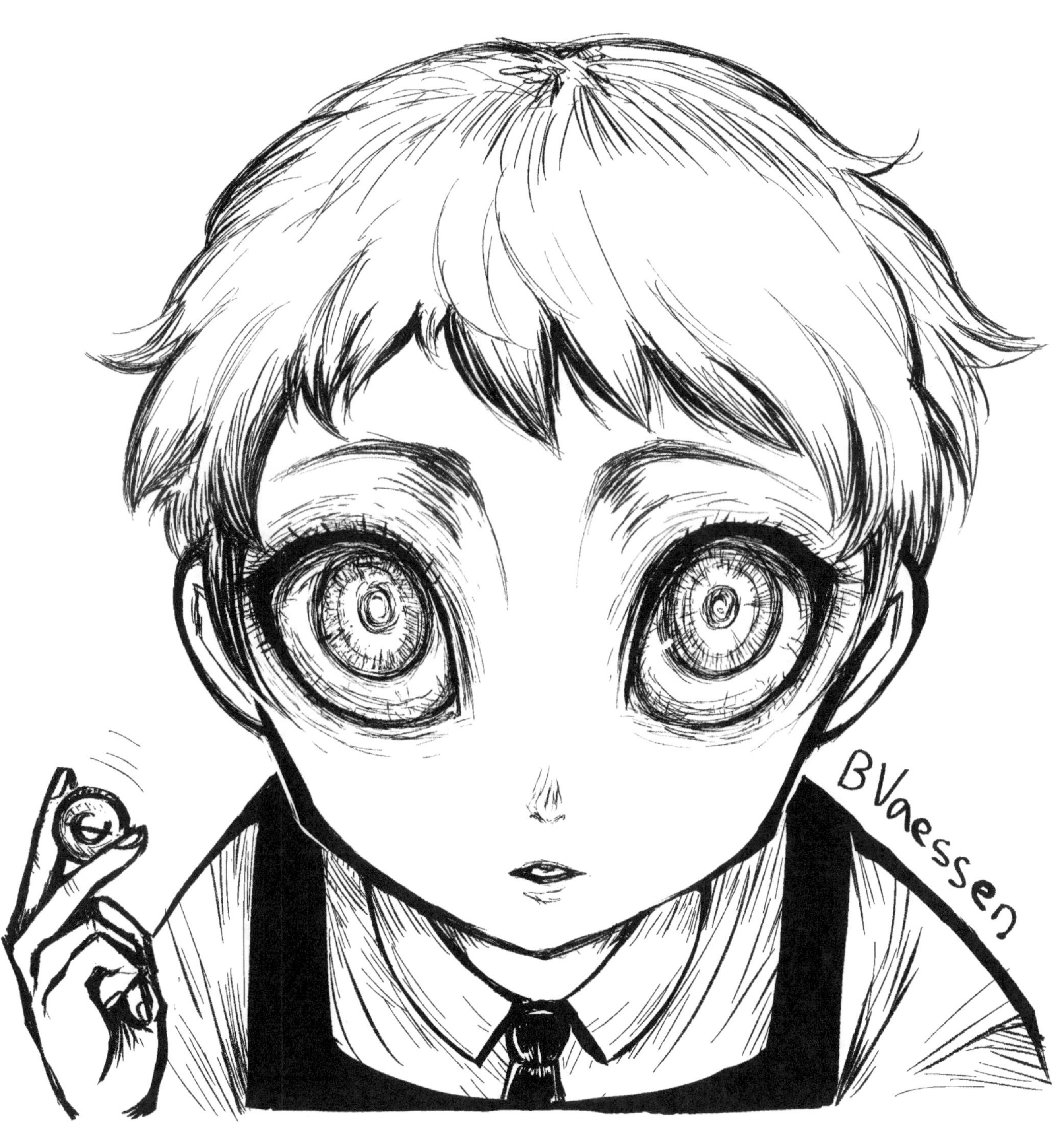

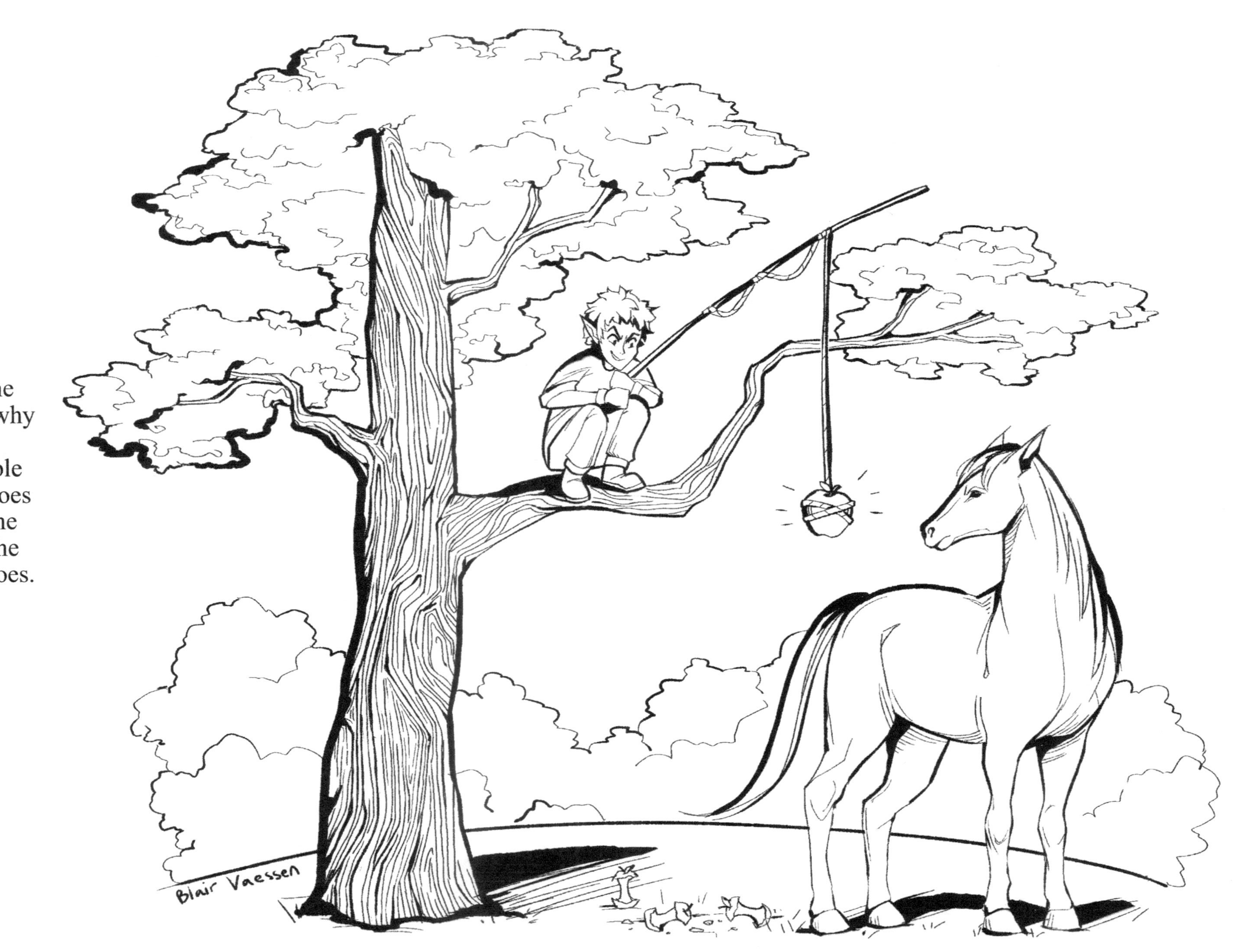

No one knows why the Unstable Hand does what he does, he just…does.

DOMENIC

Domenic has enjoyed a life long love of fantasy and horror and the subsequent art that goes along with it. His previous credits include environment and monster artwork for "Godzilla: Save the Earth Melee". You can access more of his art and projects at artstation.com/domenicbetters.

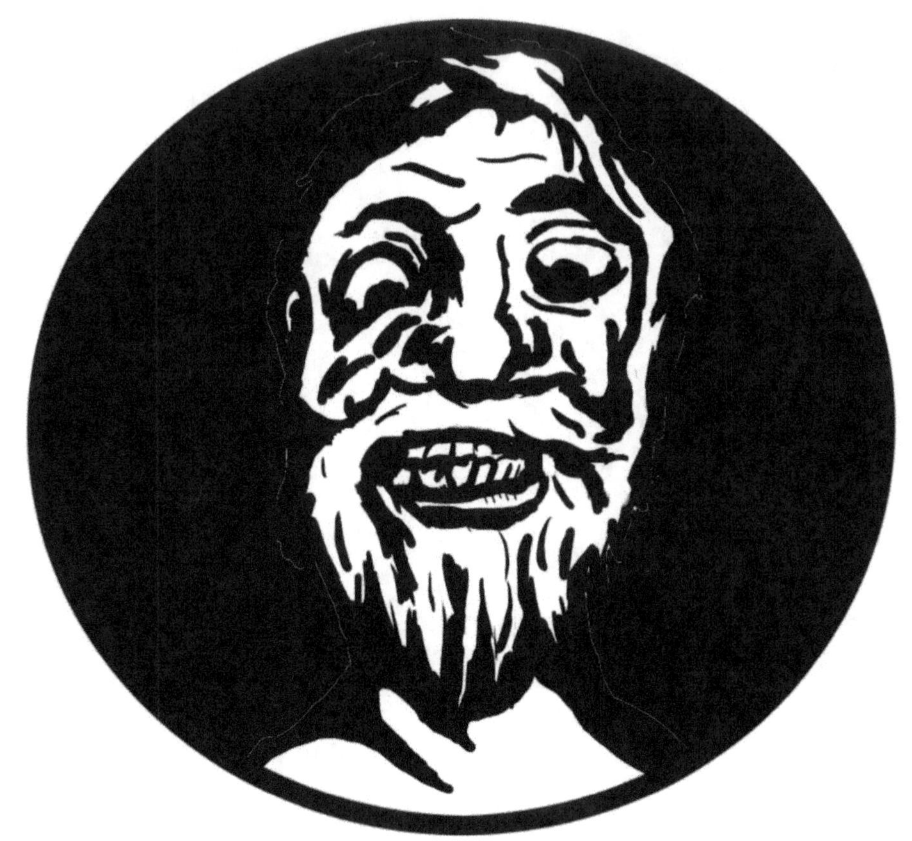

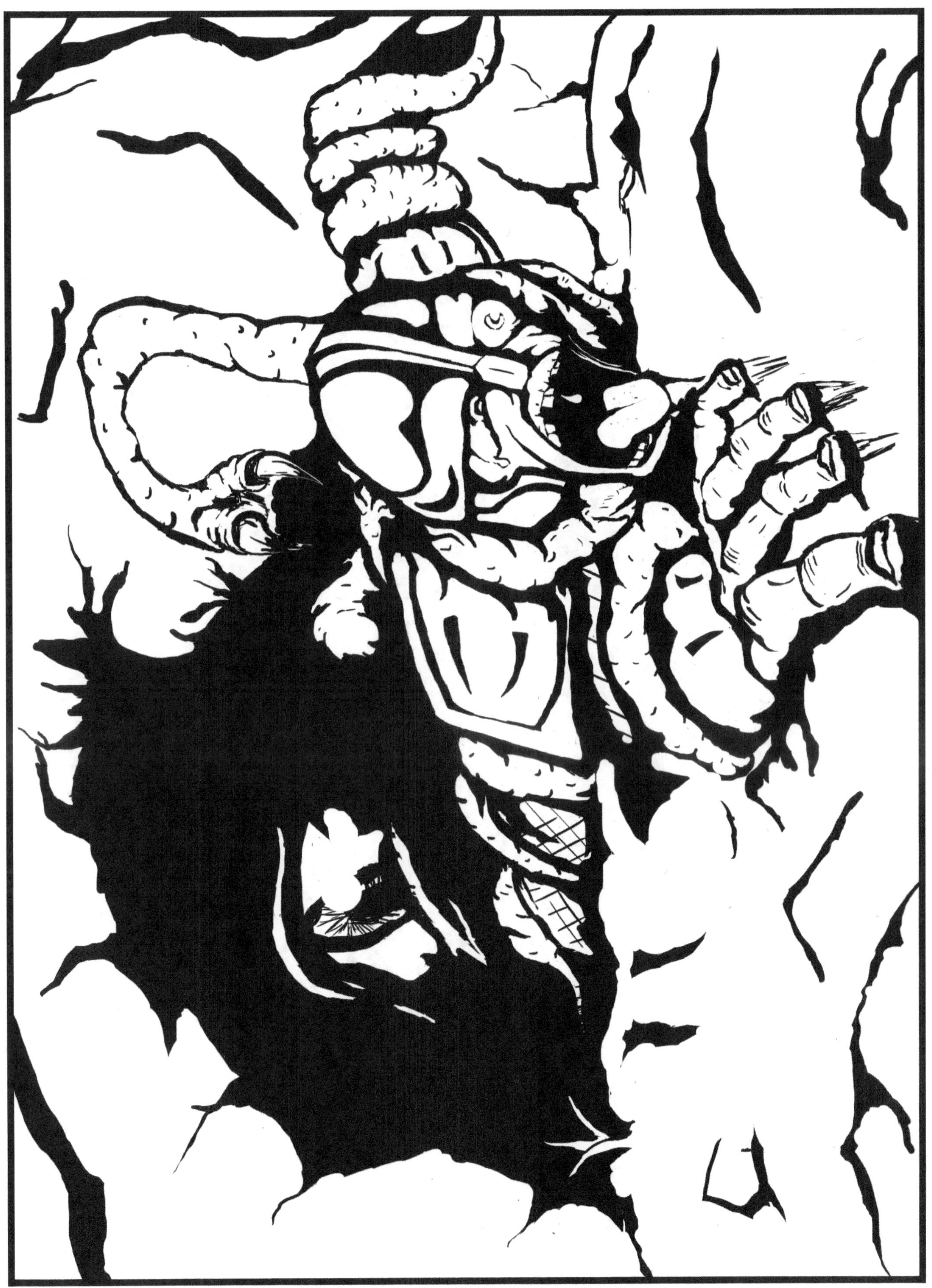

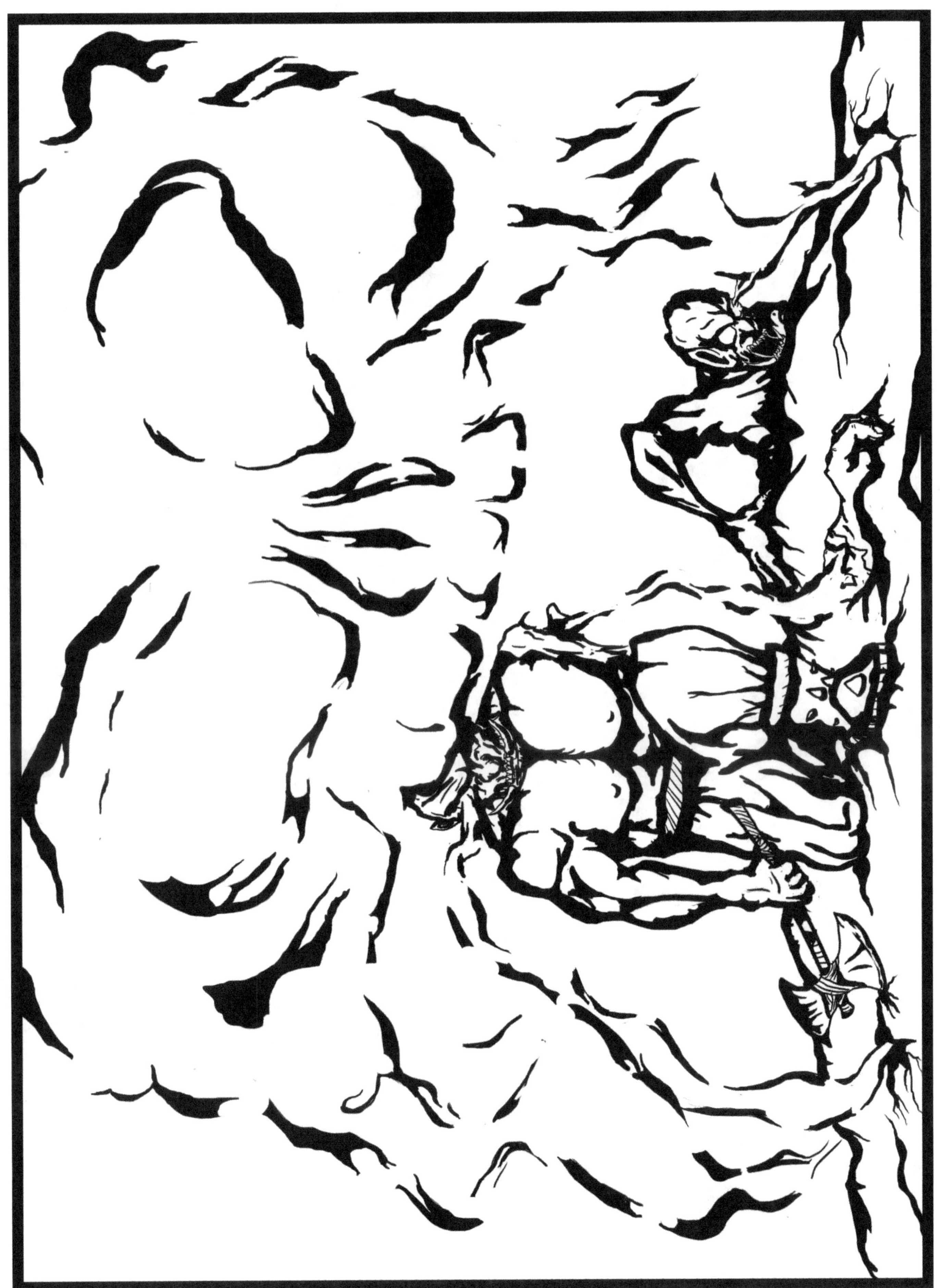

MATT

Matt Flint is a self taught artist born in Hornell, NY. Starting from an early age, Matt has been drawing for as long as he remembers. Taking his love of art, comics, anime and more, he's blended all of his influences together to create a unique style that can fit almost anywhere and in any medium. In more recent years, he's been published as a novel cover artist, comic book cover artist and comic interior artist. You can gain access to his portfolio through his website, theartofmattflint.com.

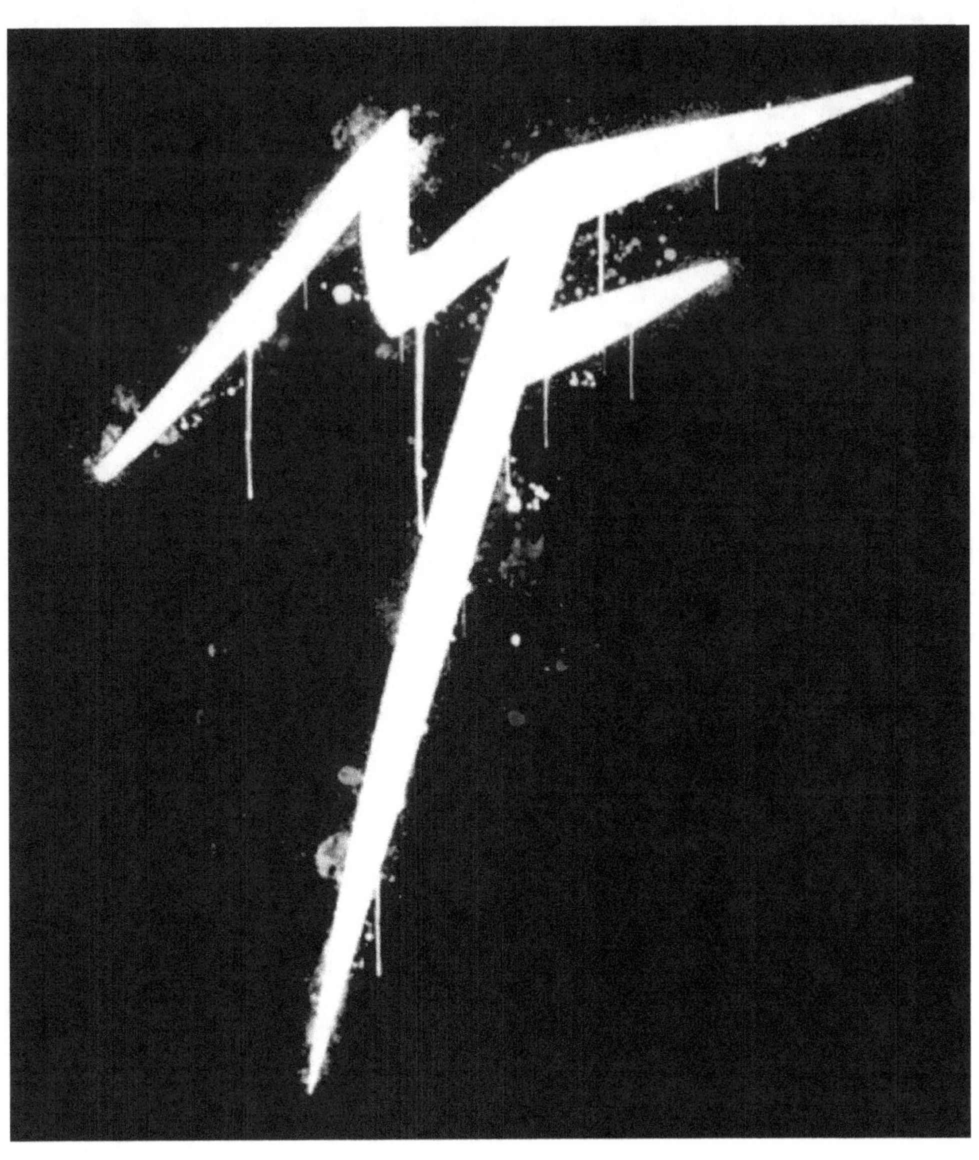

The black magic woman has a terrifying power!
Steer clear, lest she turn you into a ravaging
monster.

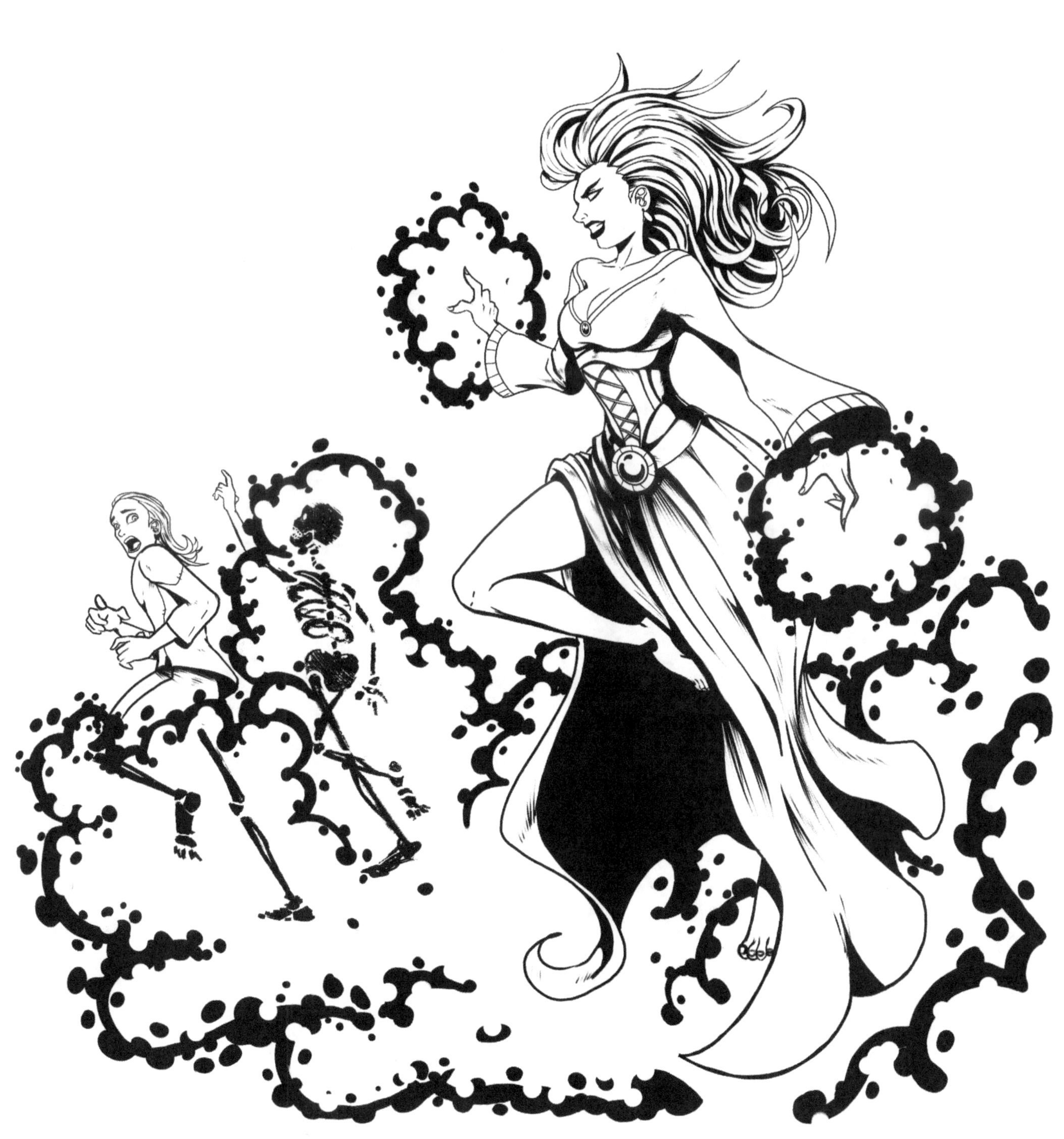

Her ravenous hunger knows no bounds! It is power
she craves. Once she gets it, she is nigh
unstoppable!

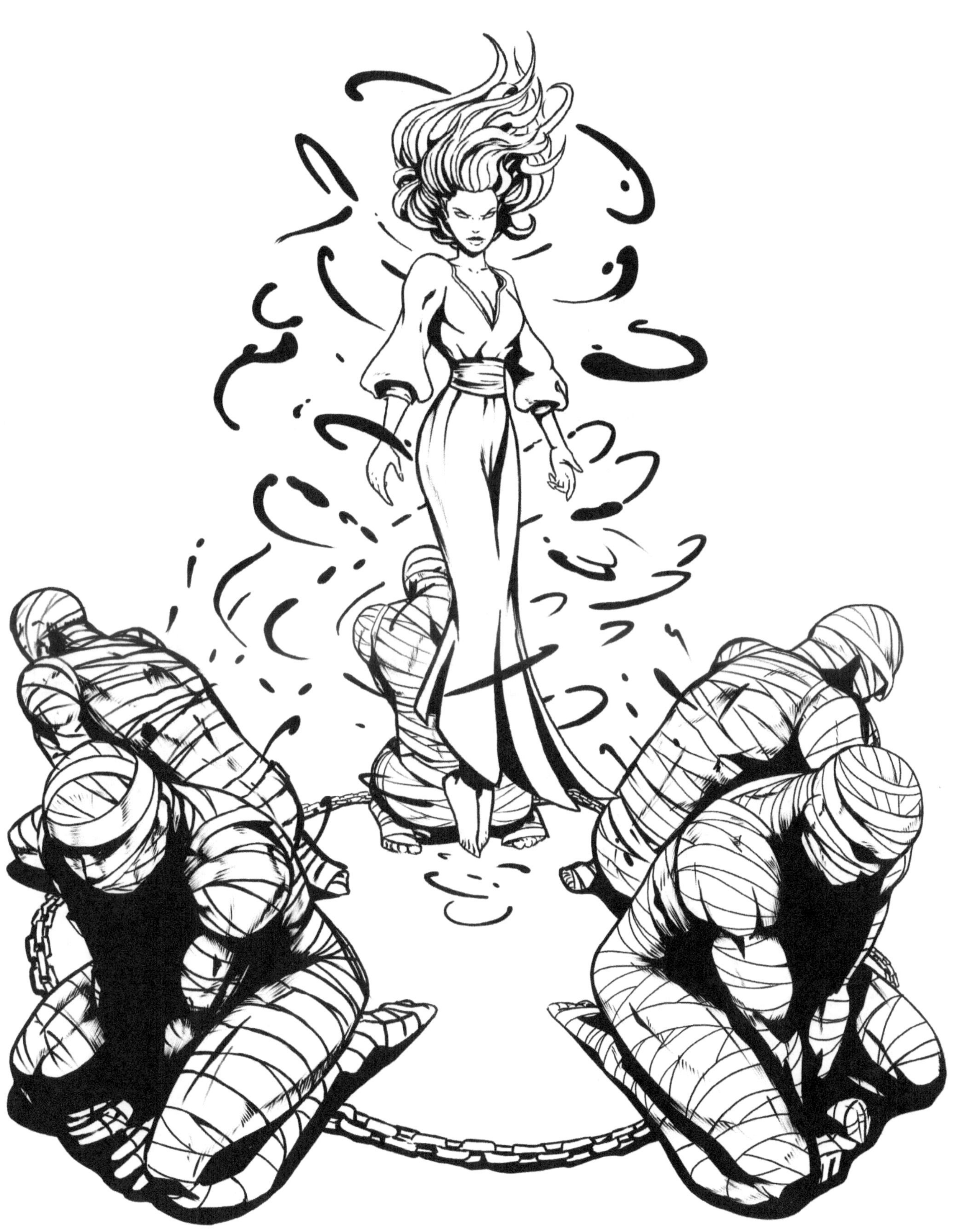

OLIVIA

Olivia is a passionate illustrator based in the Chicagoland area who lives and breathes all things magical. With a BFA in illustration and an extensive background in graphic design, Olivia brings a unique and adventurous perspective to every project she takes on. When she's not busy working on D&D character portraits or spot art for RPG rulebooks, you'll often find her nose-deep in a new fantasy novel, roaming the halls of the latest comic convention in full costume, or cuddling with her dogs in the middle of a Lord of the Rings marathon. You can follow Olivia's unexpected journey through her instagram page: instagram.com/mangamimi15.

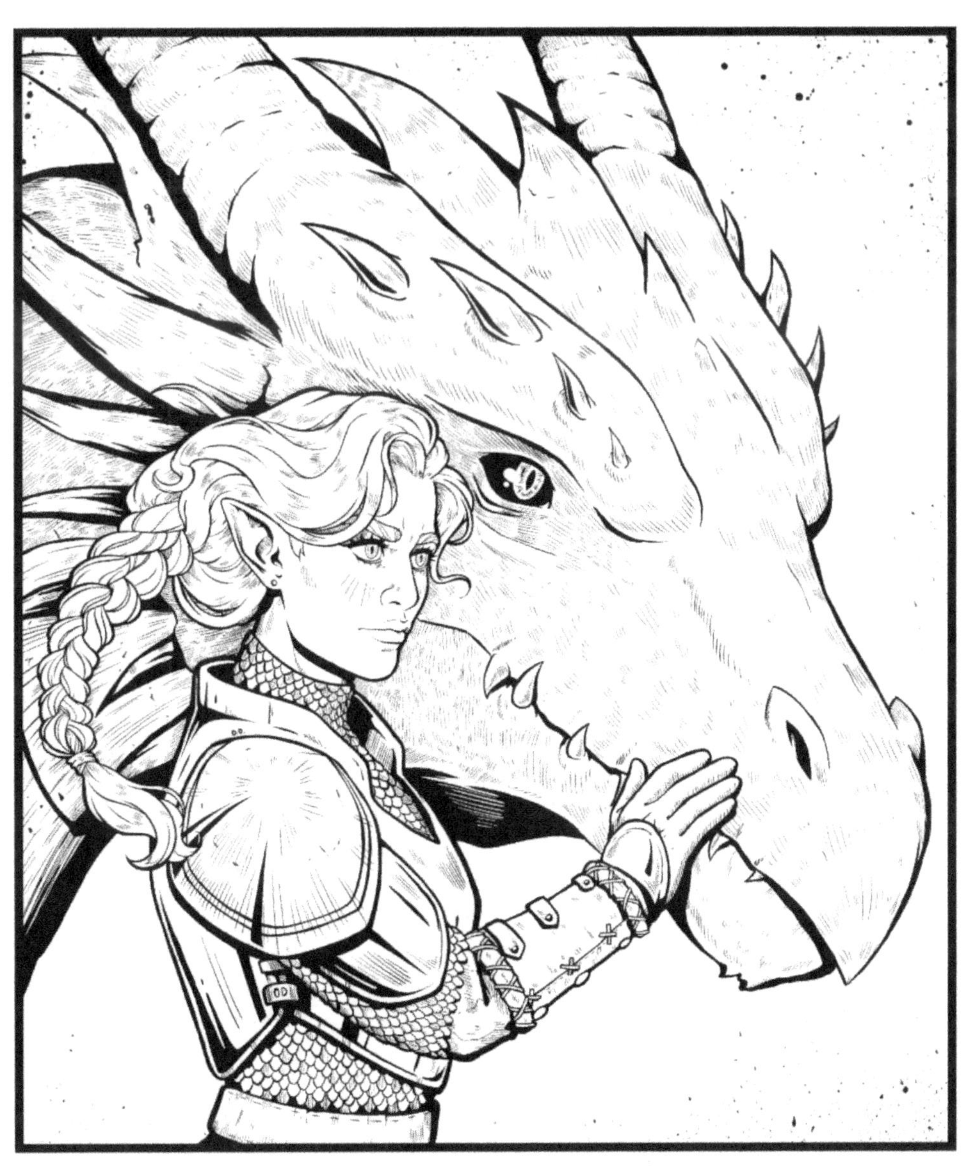

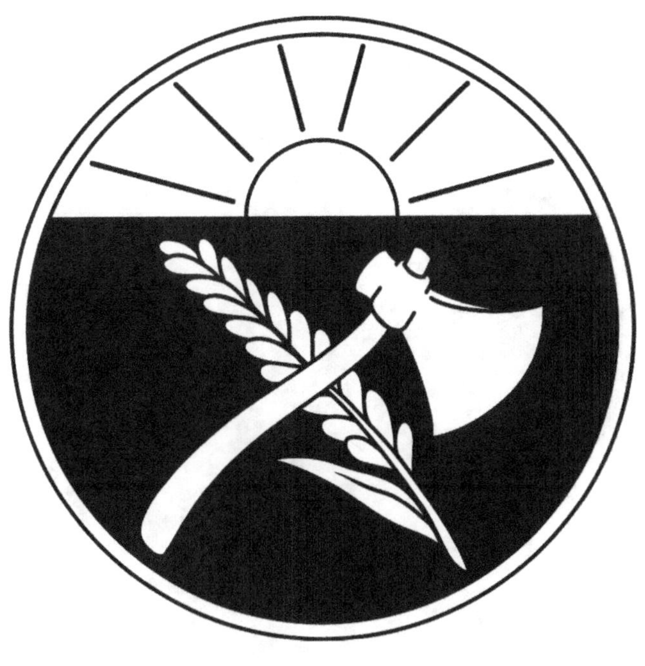

Ministry of Founding

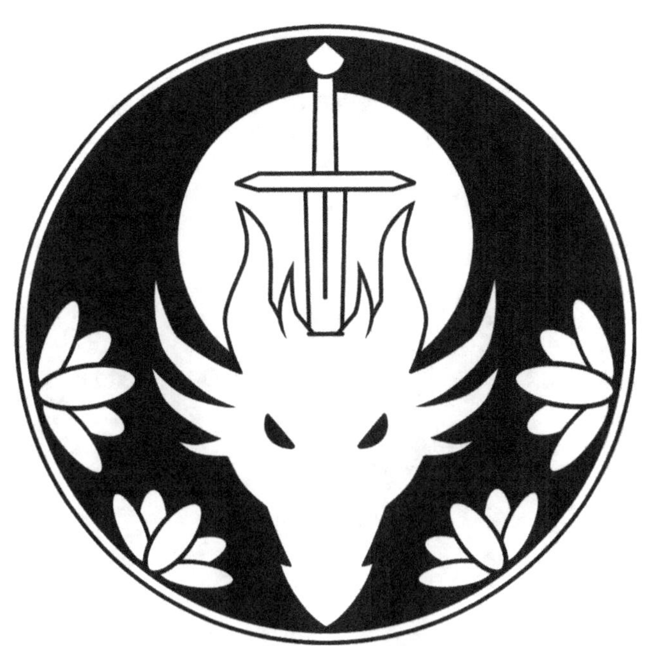

Pursuants

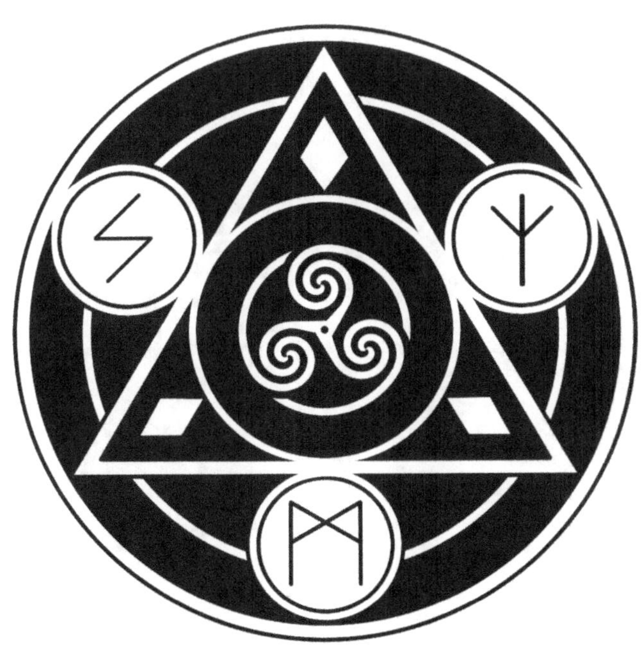

Arcanum Ministorum

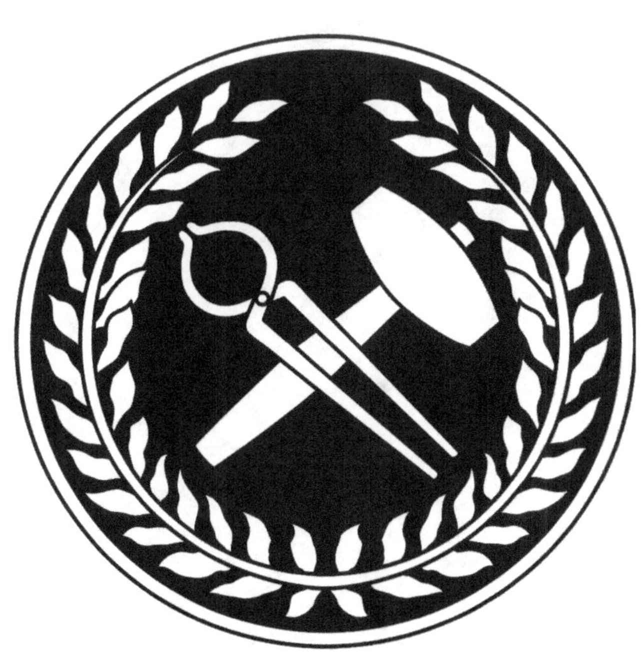

Artisans Circle

Mr. Ball Legs is not going to be happy that you've eaten his friends.

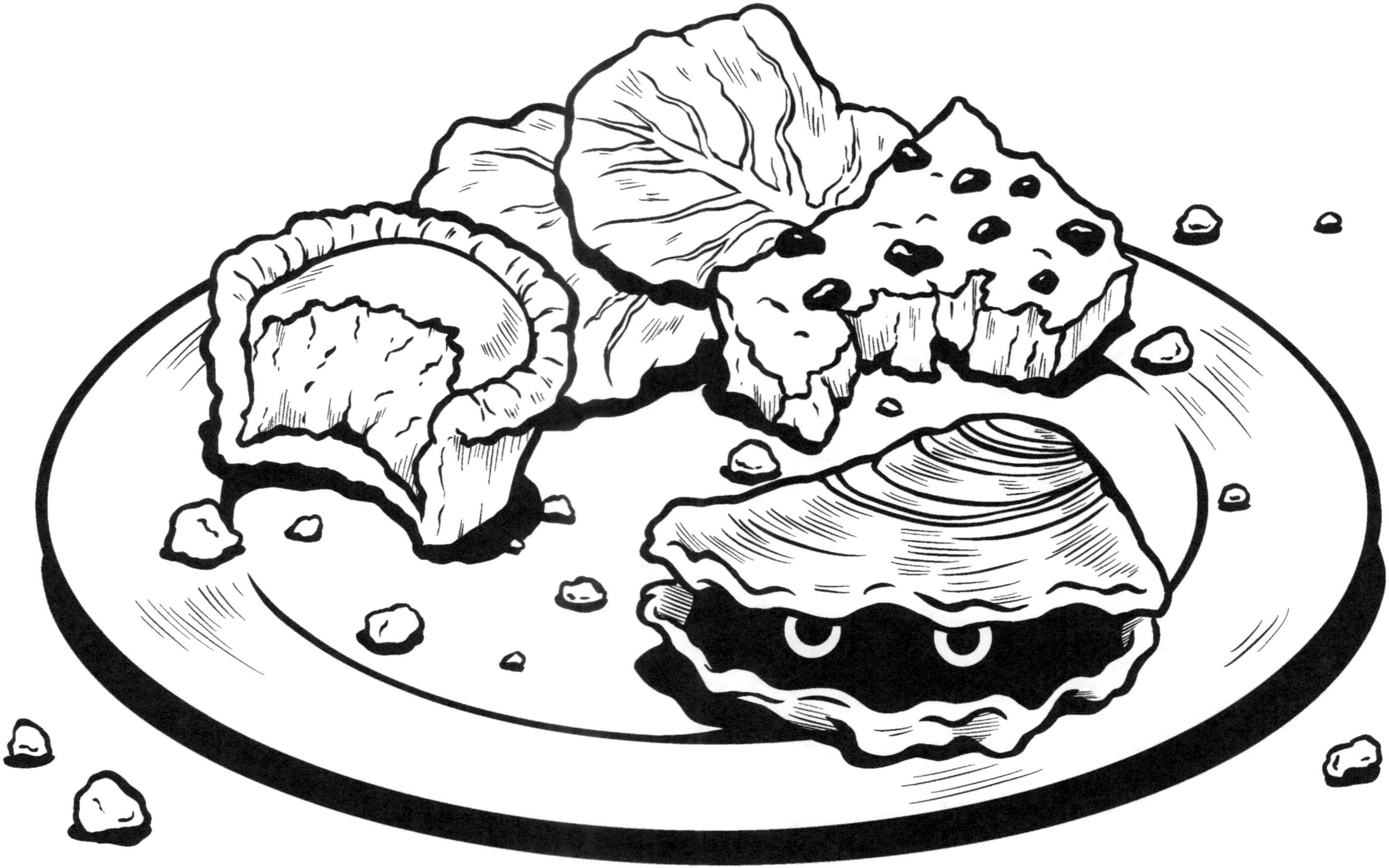

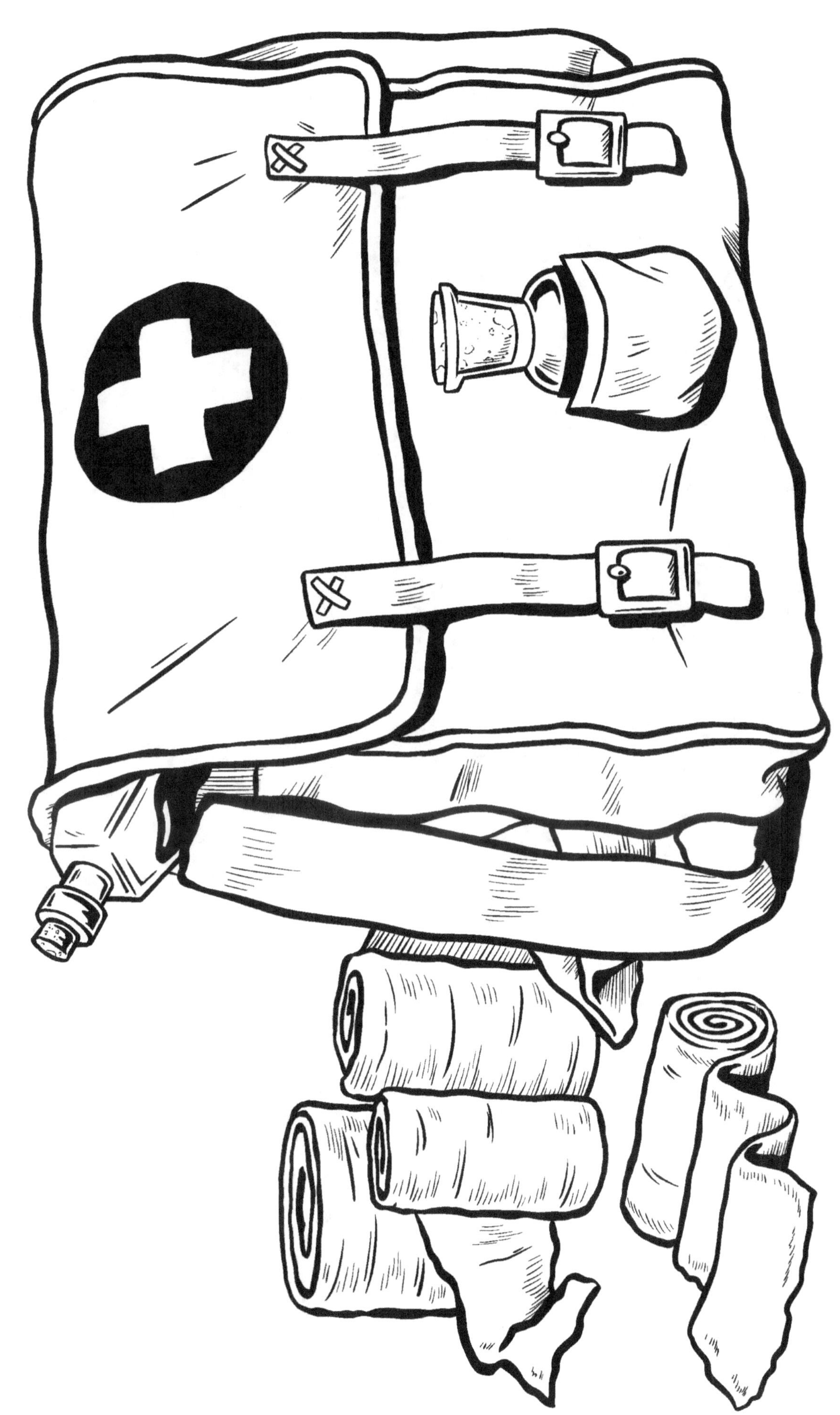

Stock up on your bandages, they really come in handy out in the field.

It's time to grab the bull by his horns.

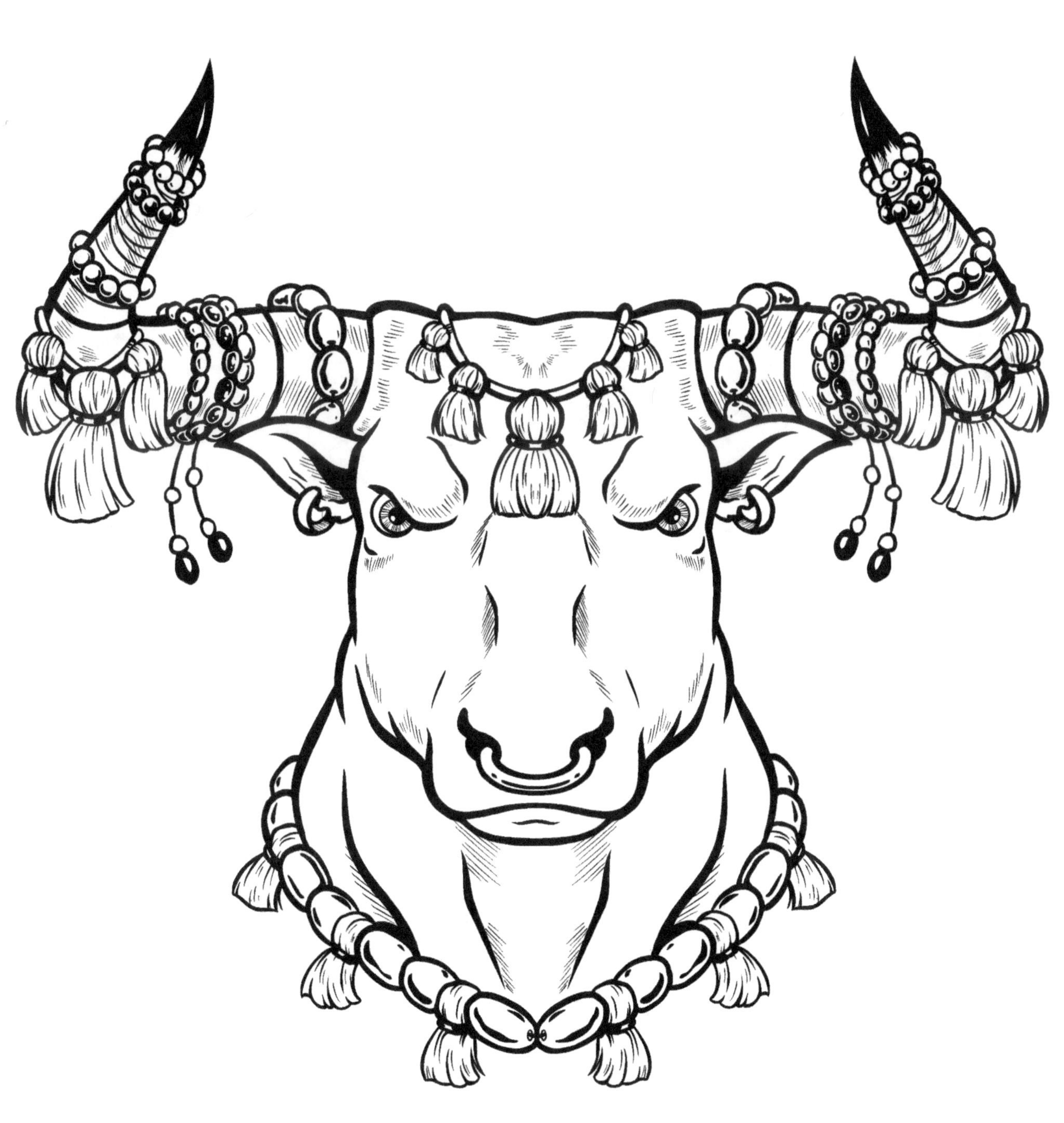

Ready the grappling hooks!

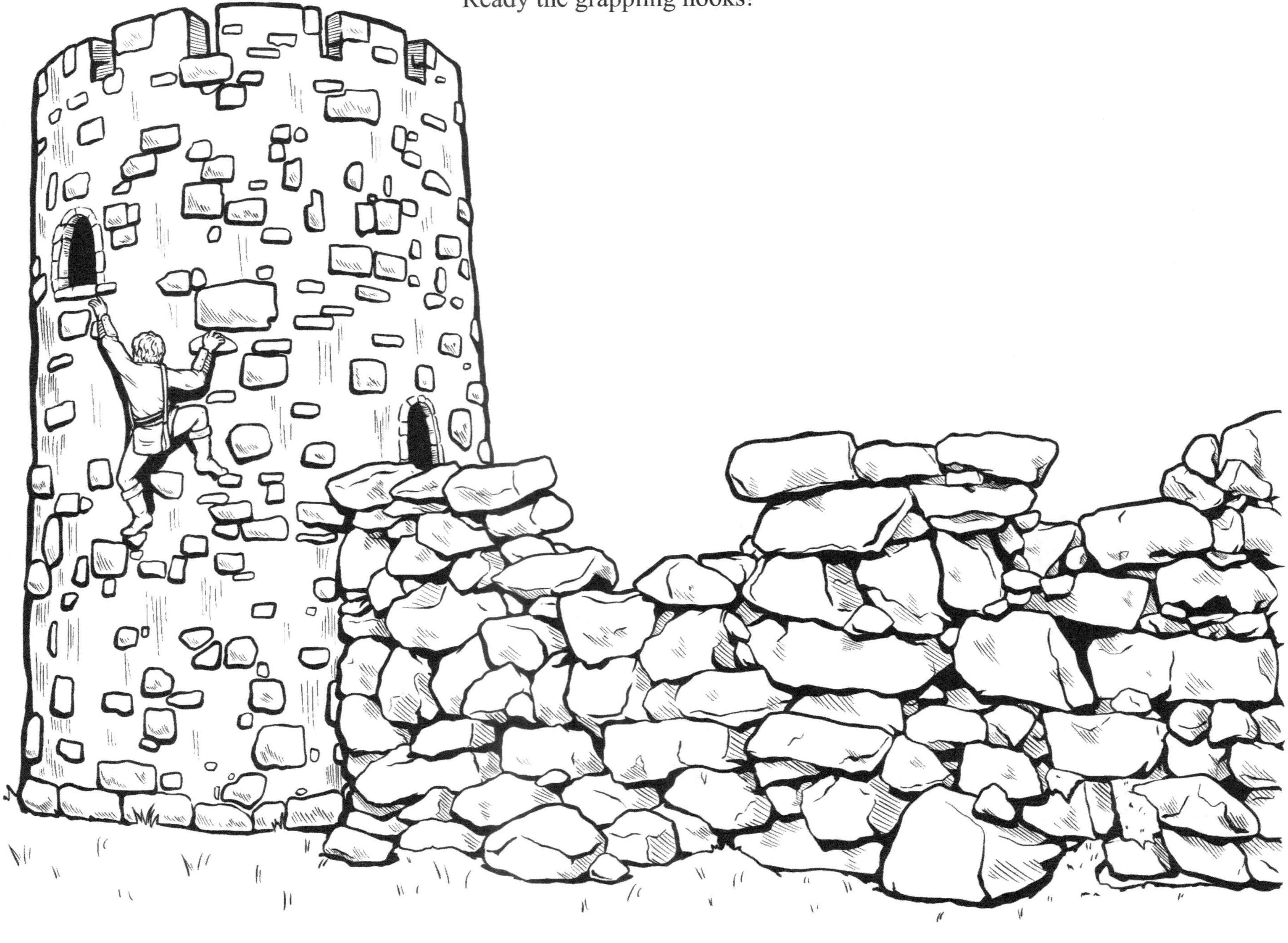

Got any Aces up your sleeve?

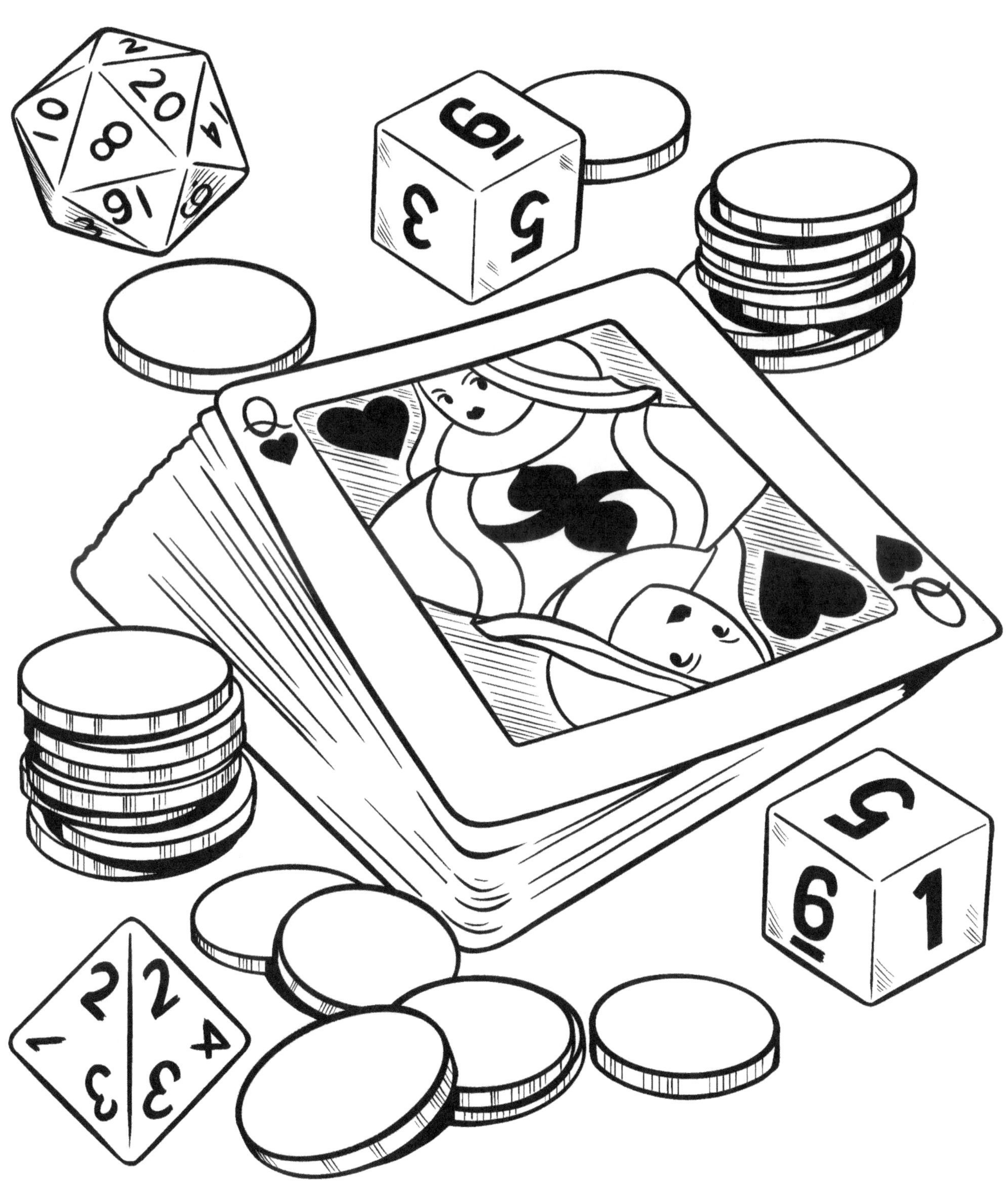

Be sure to stop by Merchants Square to grab some gear!

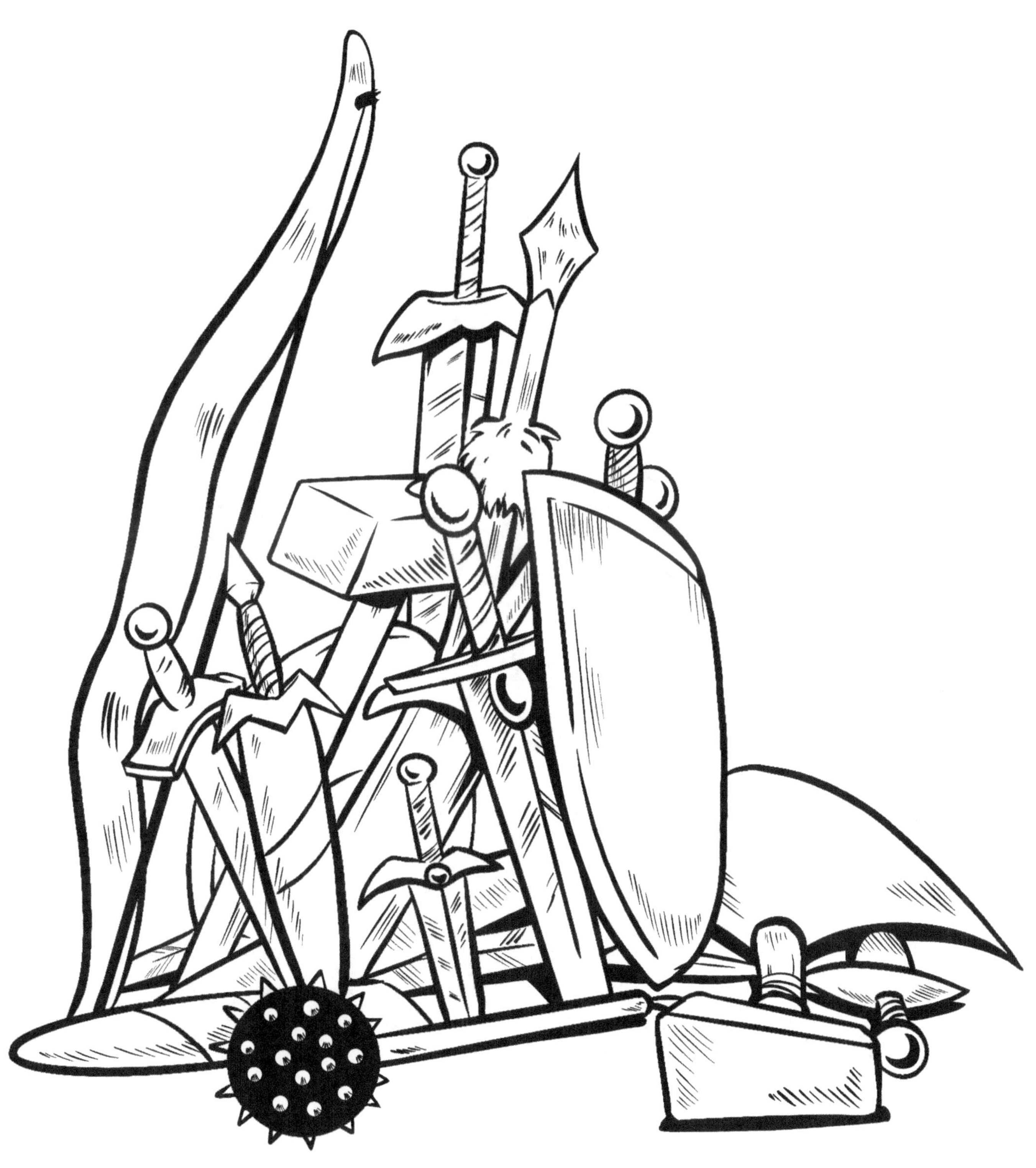

When I asked you to give me a hand with this…oh, nevermind.

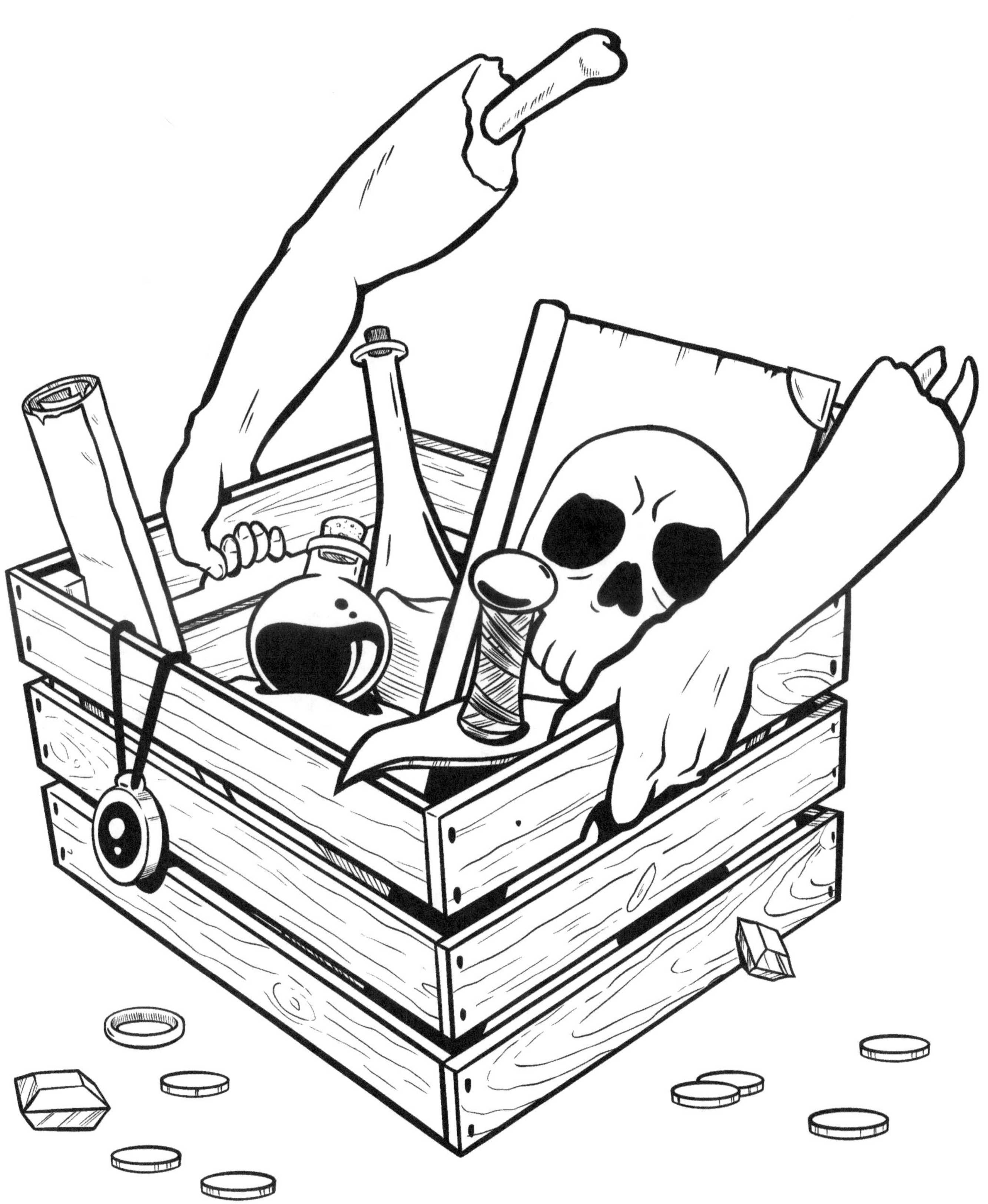

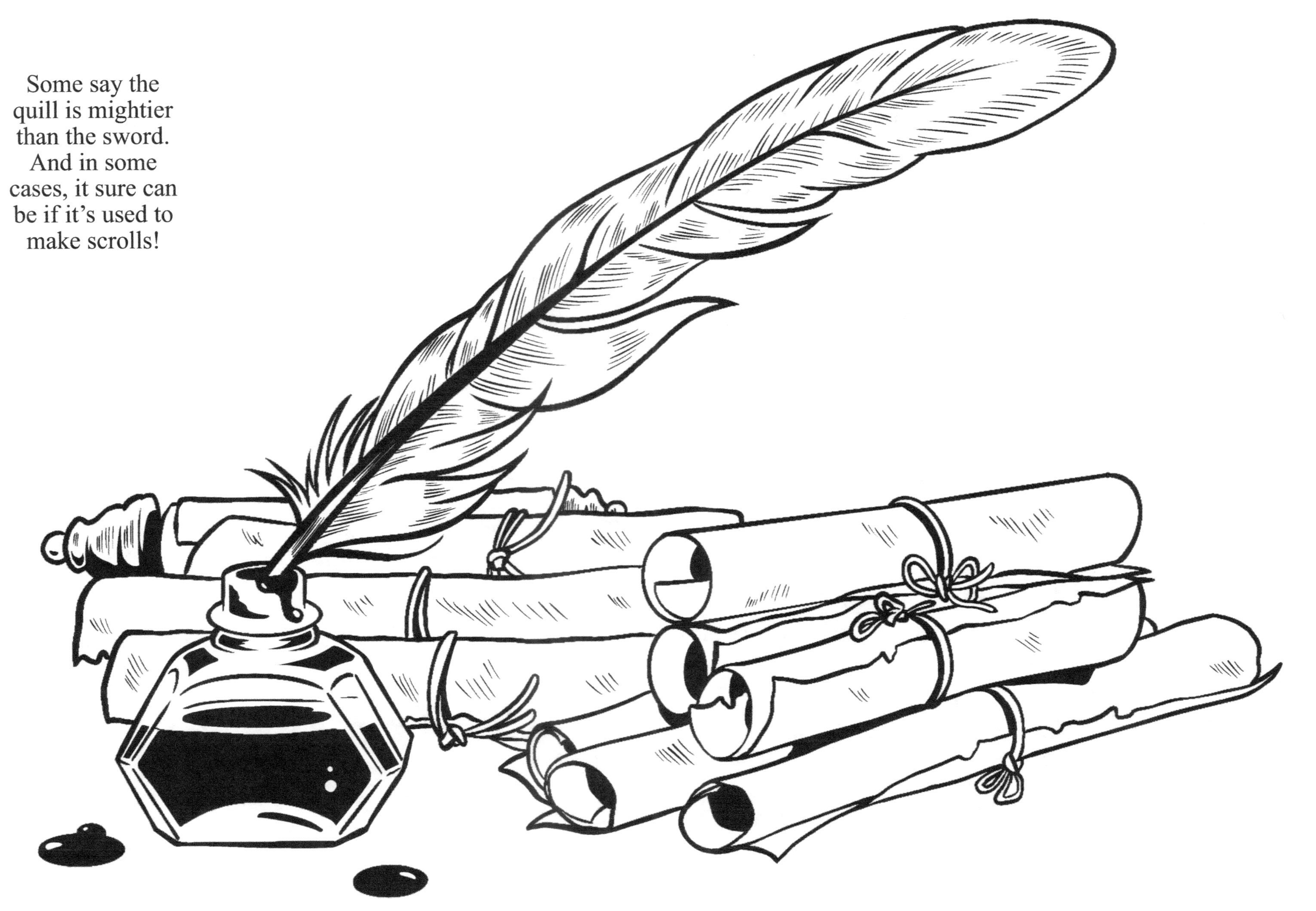

Some say the
quill is mightier
than the sword.
And in some
cases, it sure can
be if it's used to
make scrolls!

When you're the Last Man Standing, the buck stops with you.

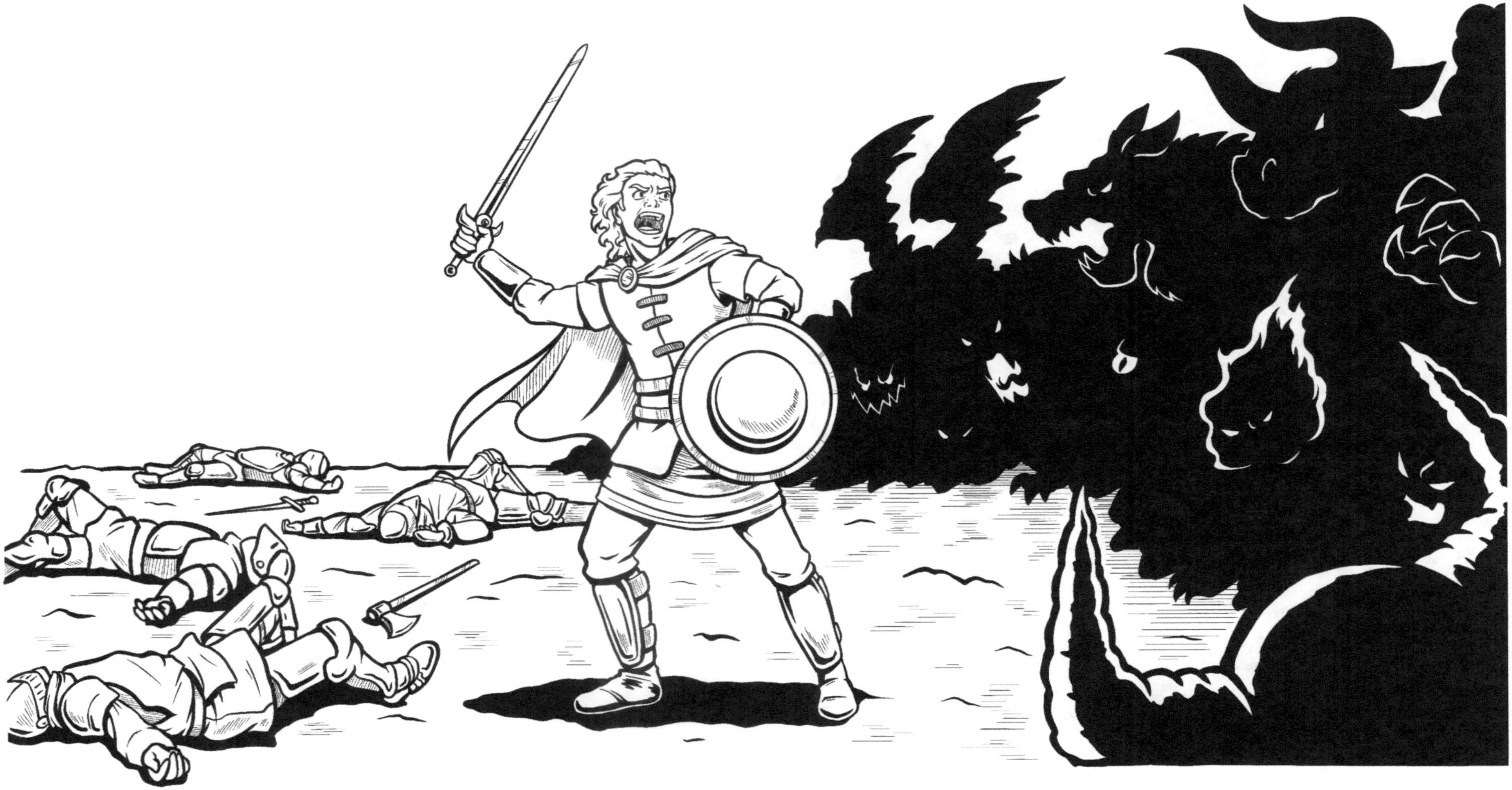

Just your typical, run-of-the-mill blood magic altar.
Just don't tell the Consortium Guard, okay?

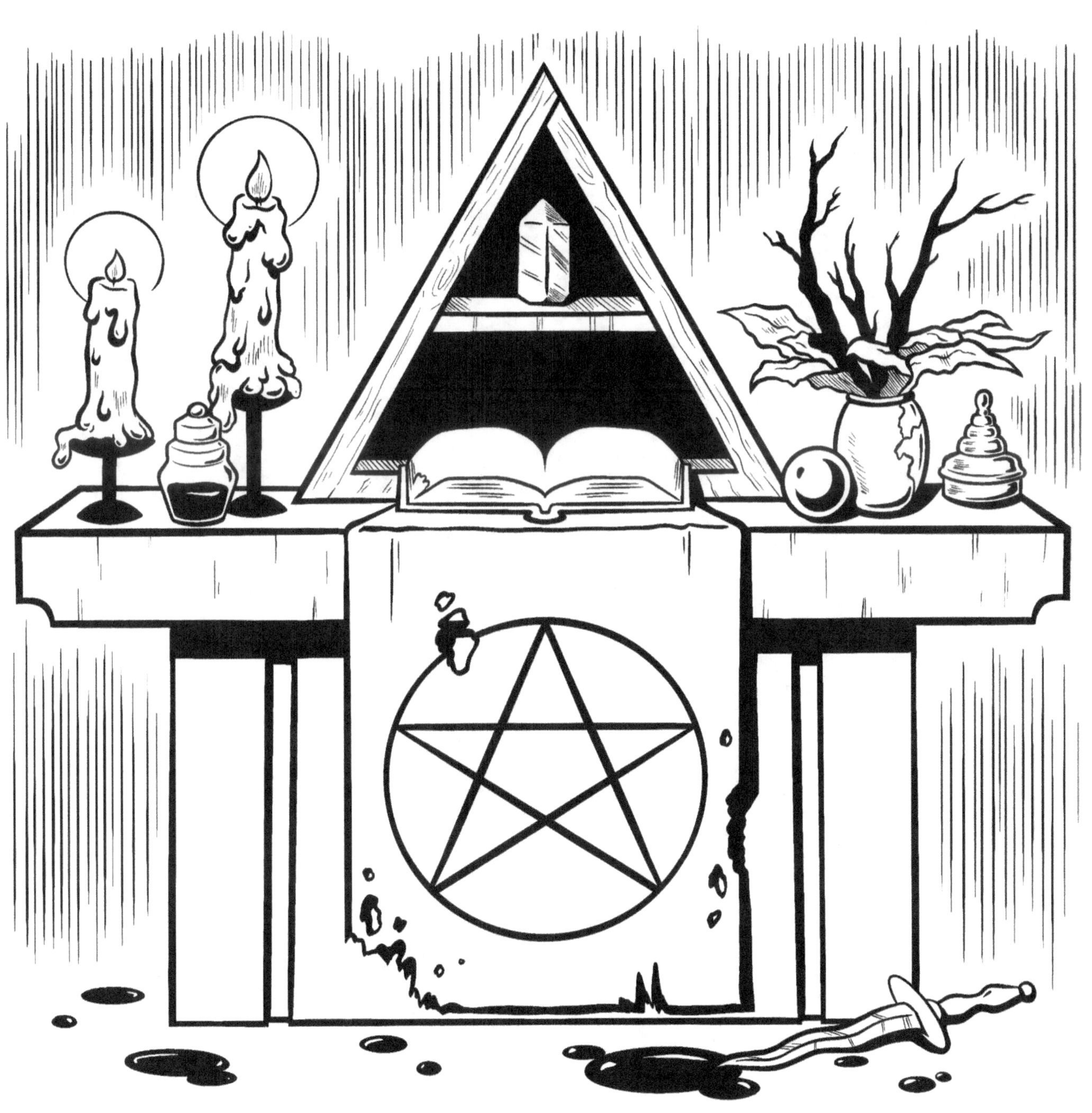

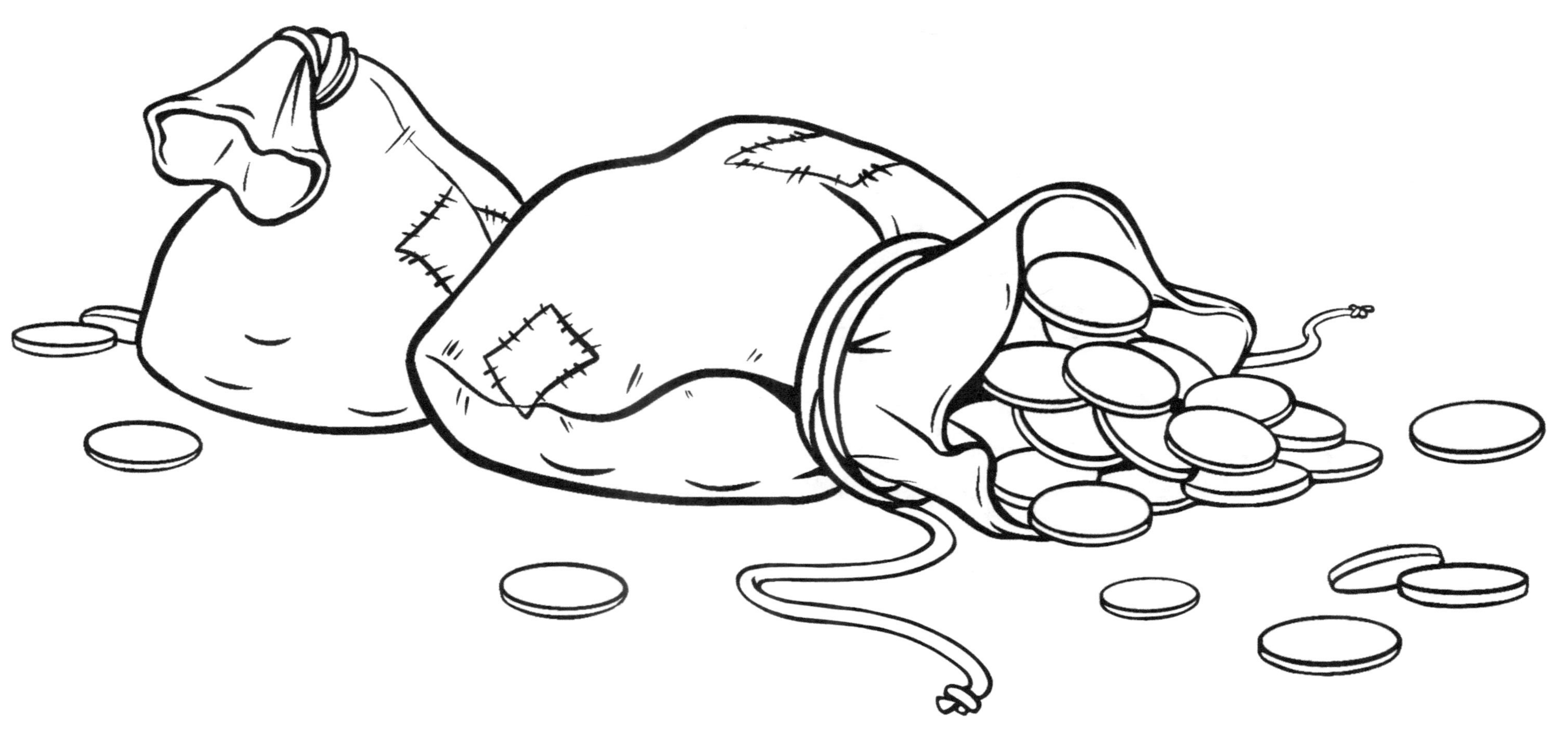

Guilder for your thoughts?

You can keep so many 10 foot poles and 50 foot lengths of rope in here!

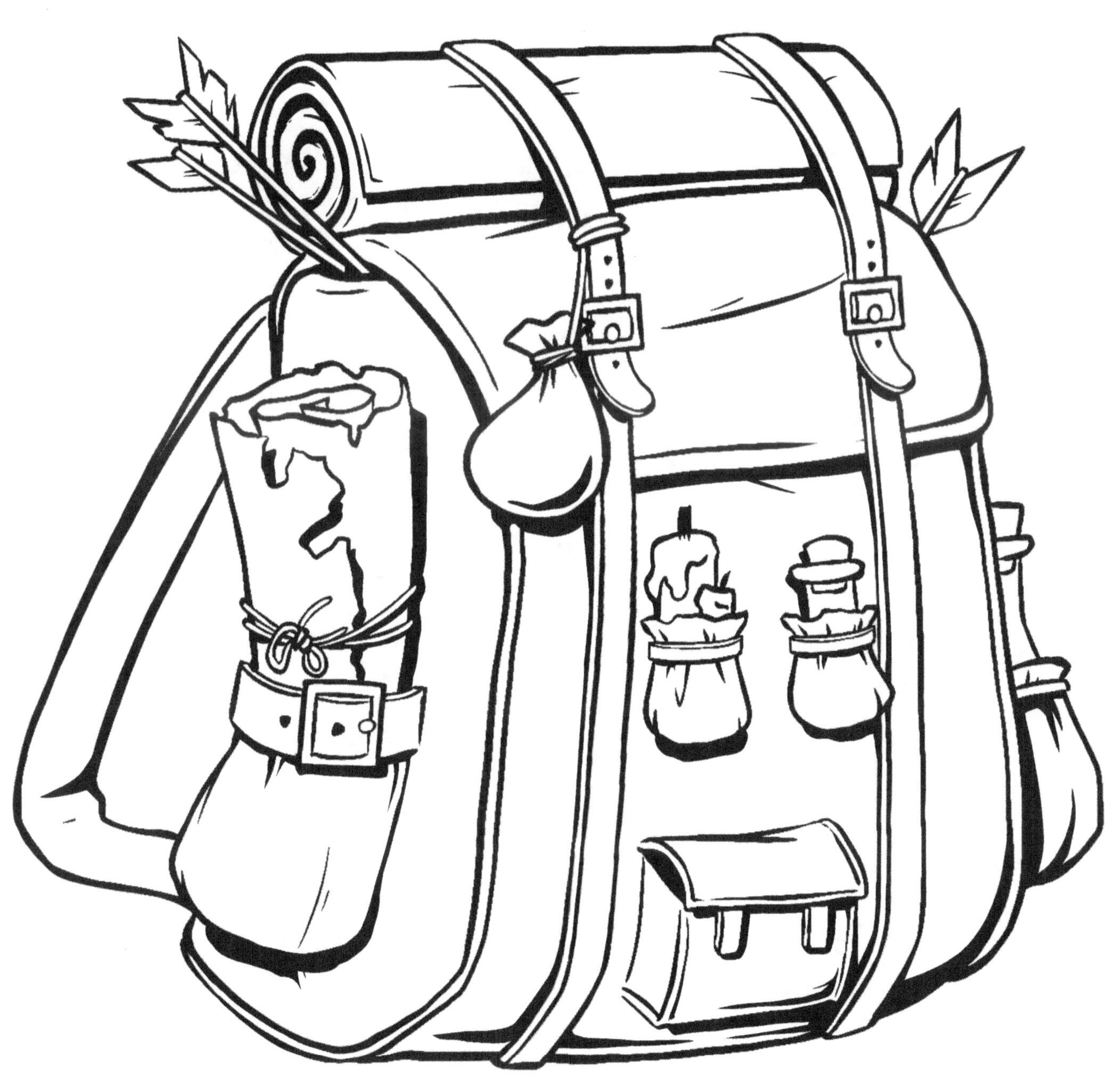

Don't lose your head over this, it's not the end of
the world. Well, maybe except for this guy.

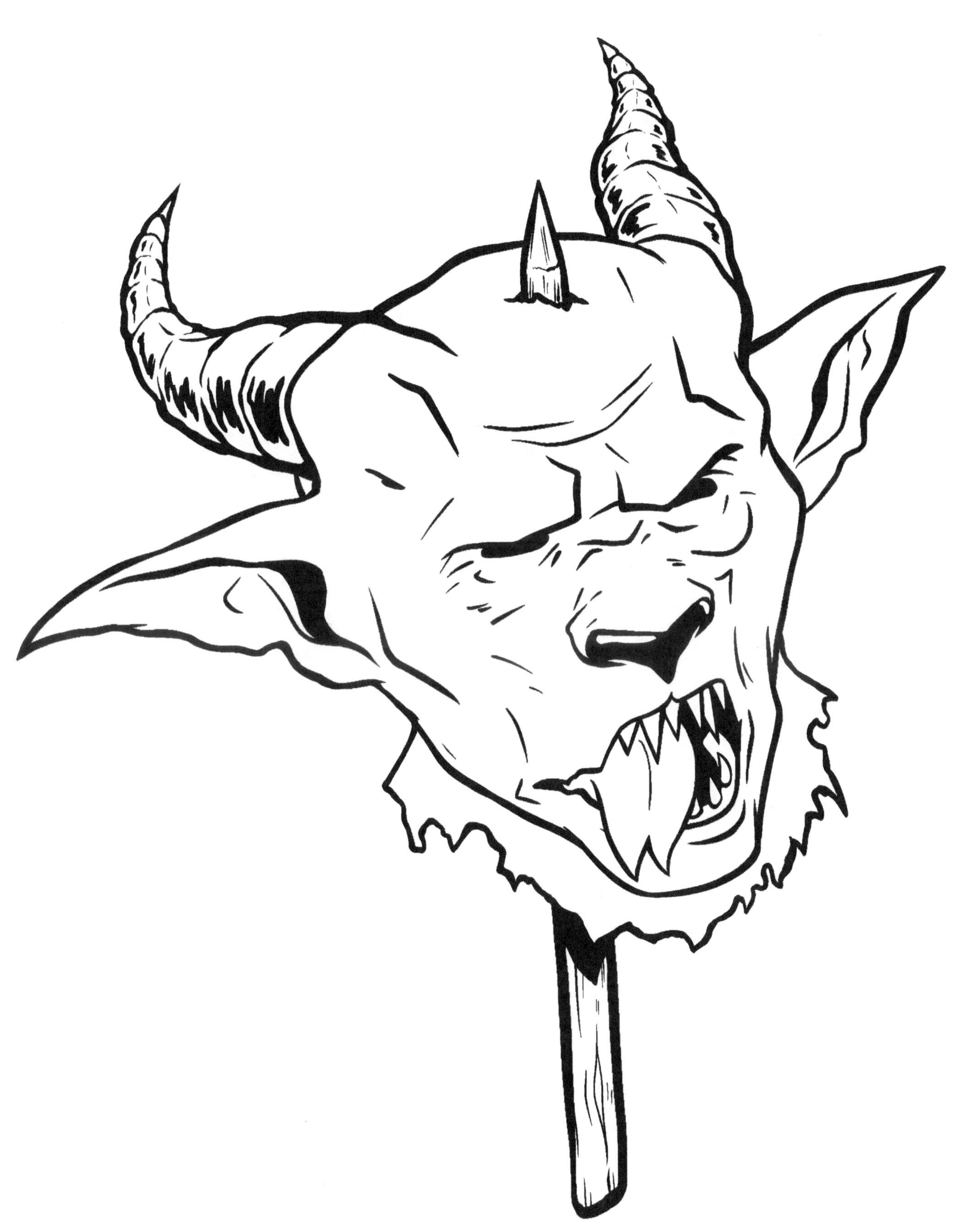

Wands for sale. Sorry, no returns.

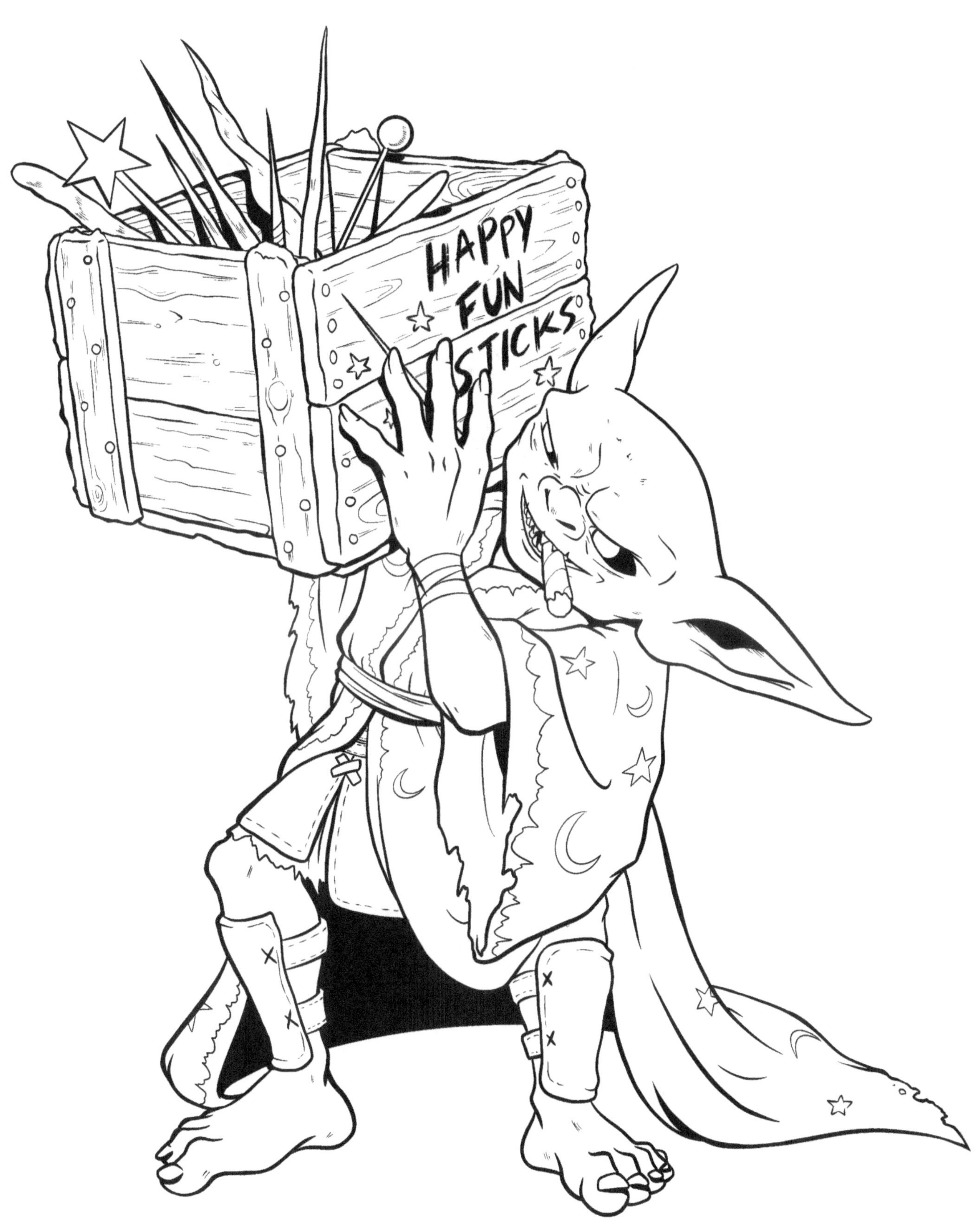

Elixirs: Use with extreme caution.

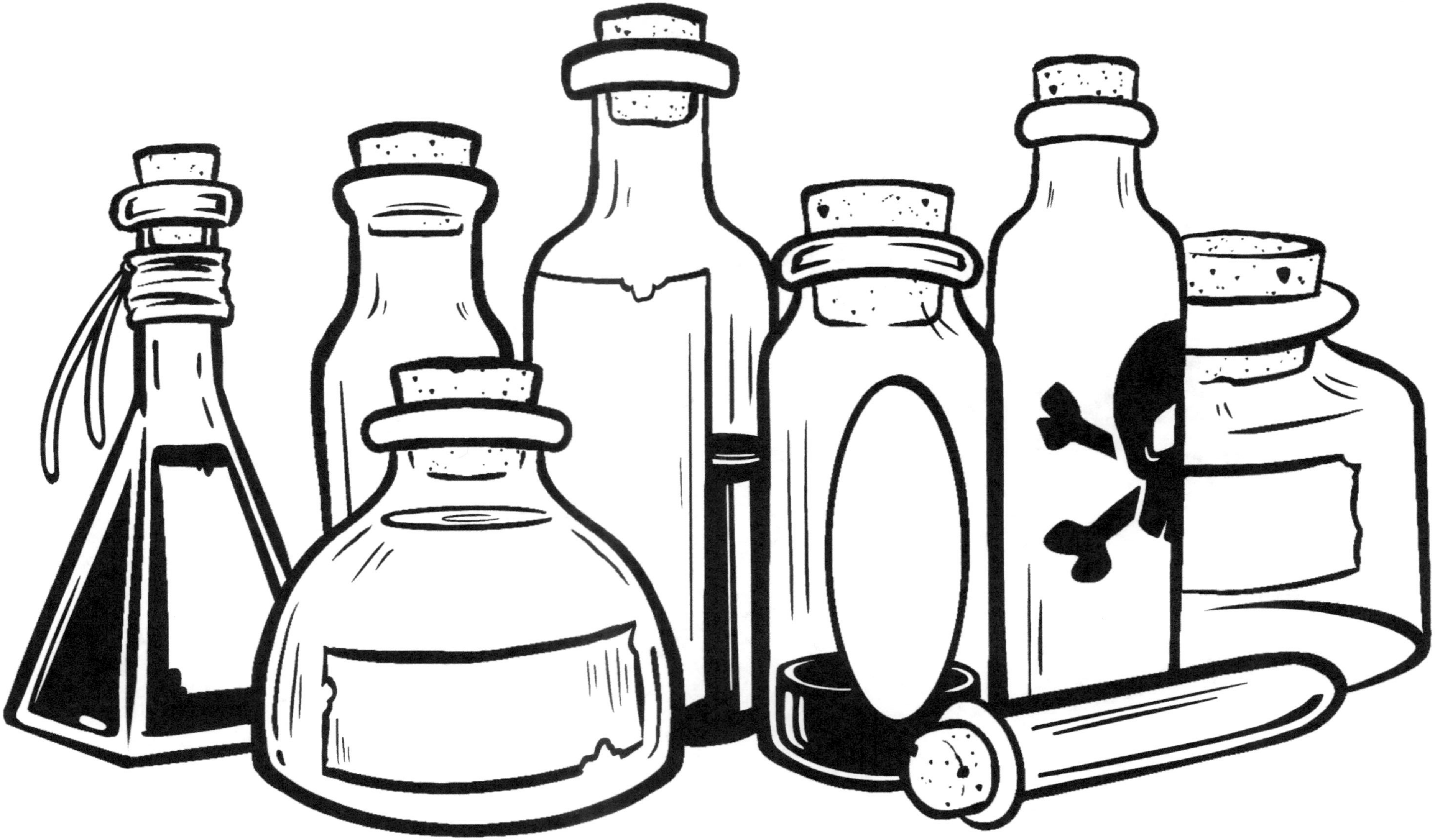

Can I keep him? Pleeeaaase?

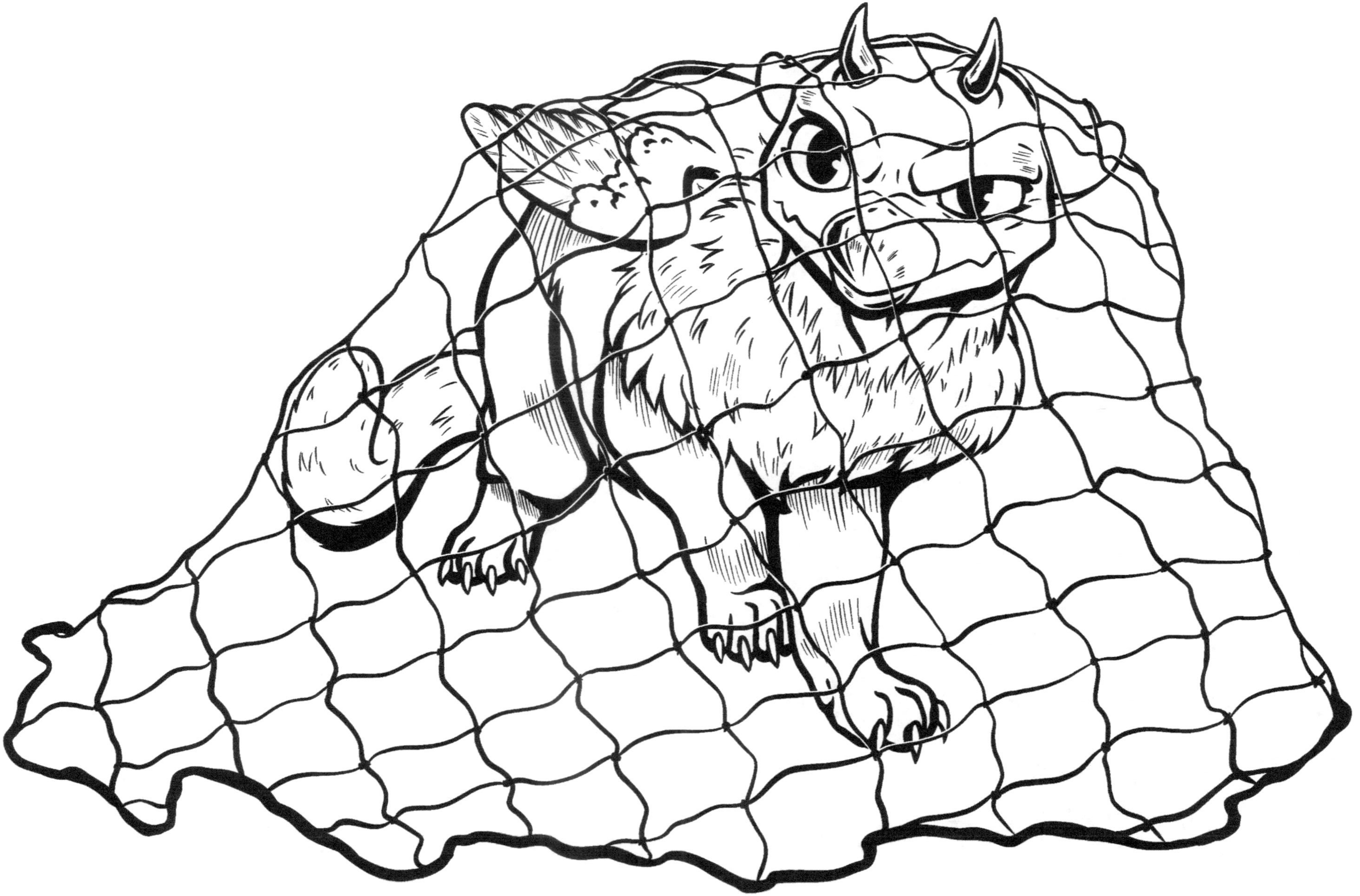

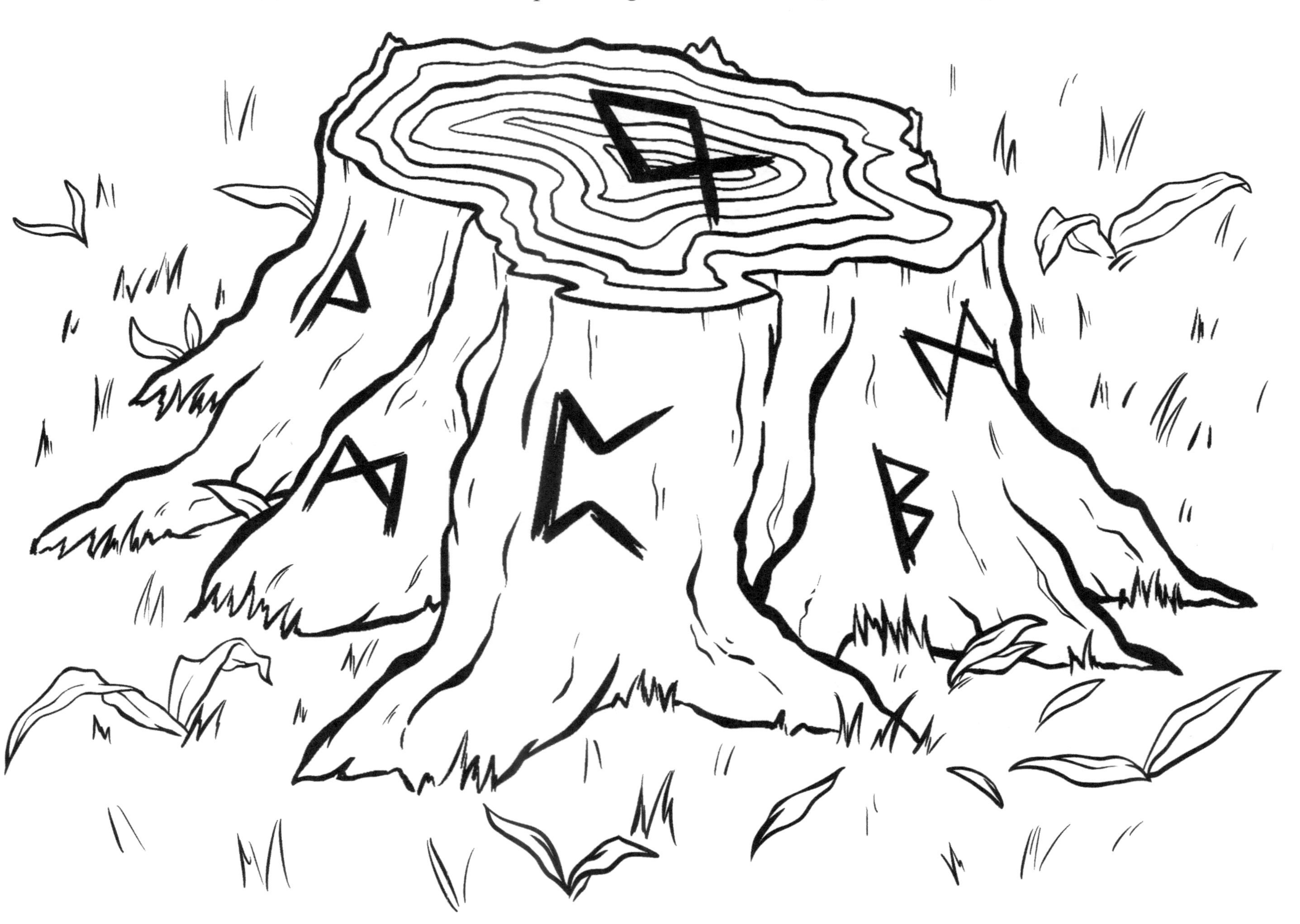

Looks like someone's been practicing their runecrafting in the forest again.

You don't have
to be pretty,
graceful, OR
limber to be a
knight. But it
sure helps.

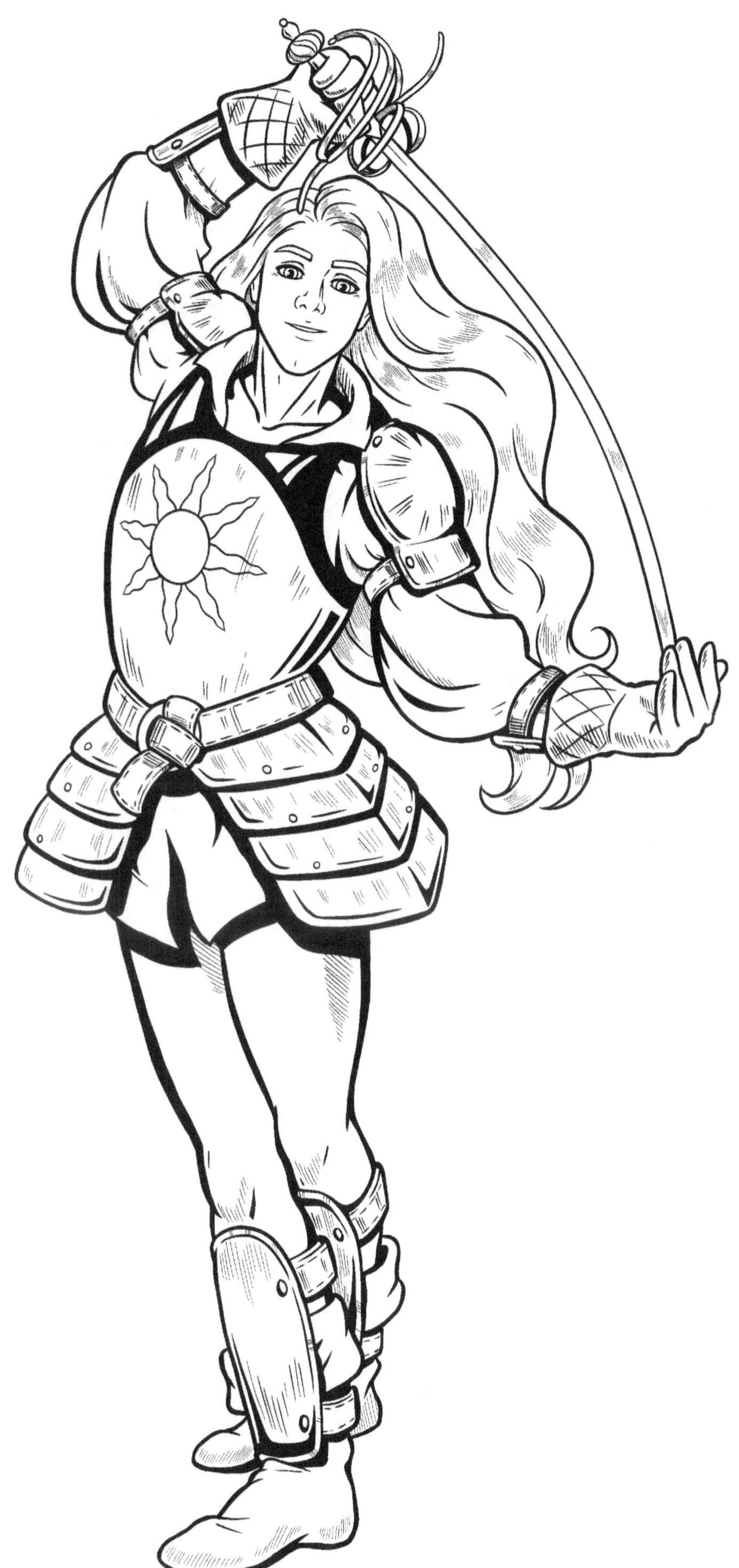

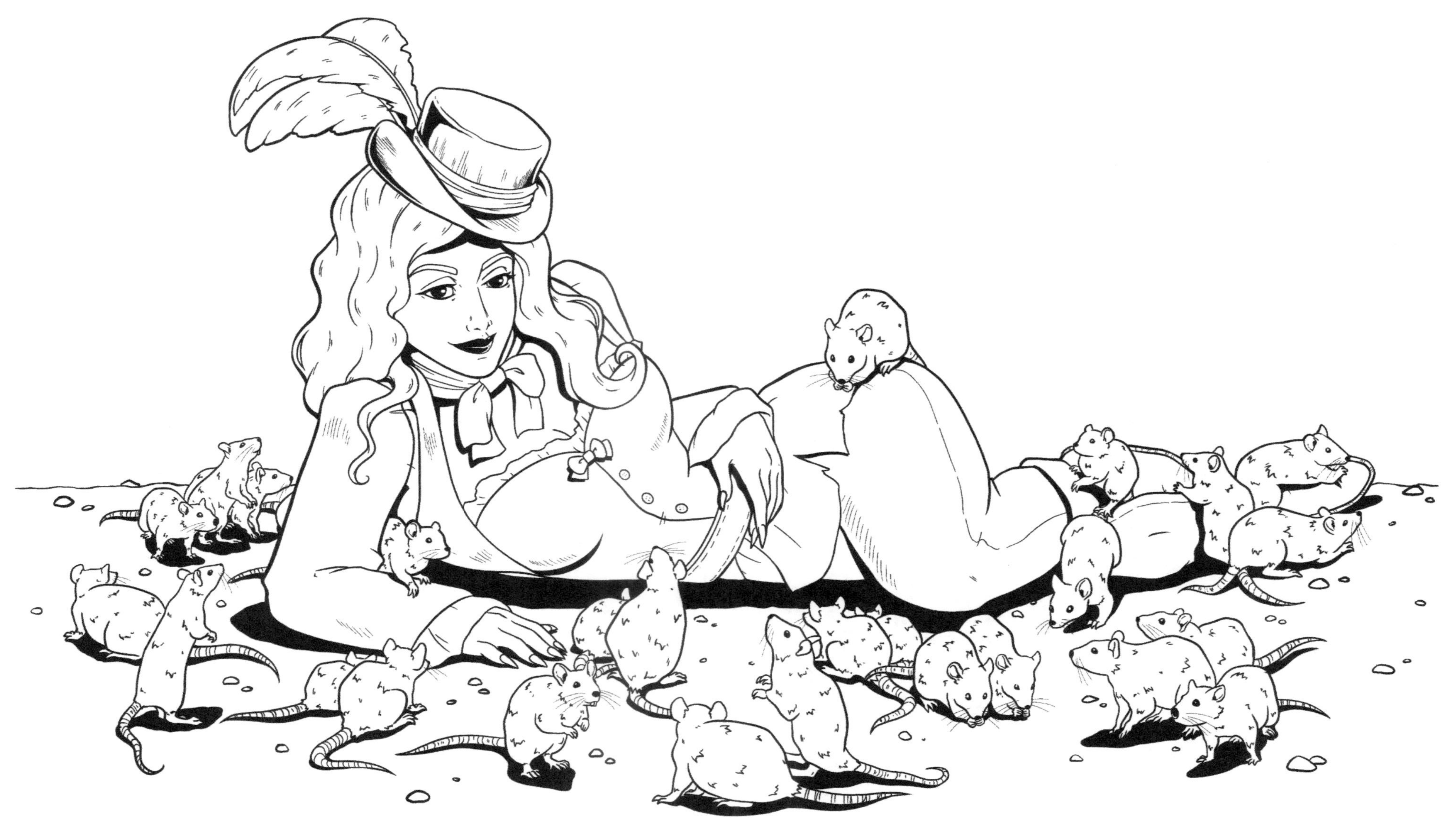

I am Vermina, Queen of the Rats.

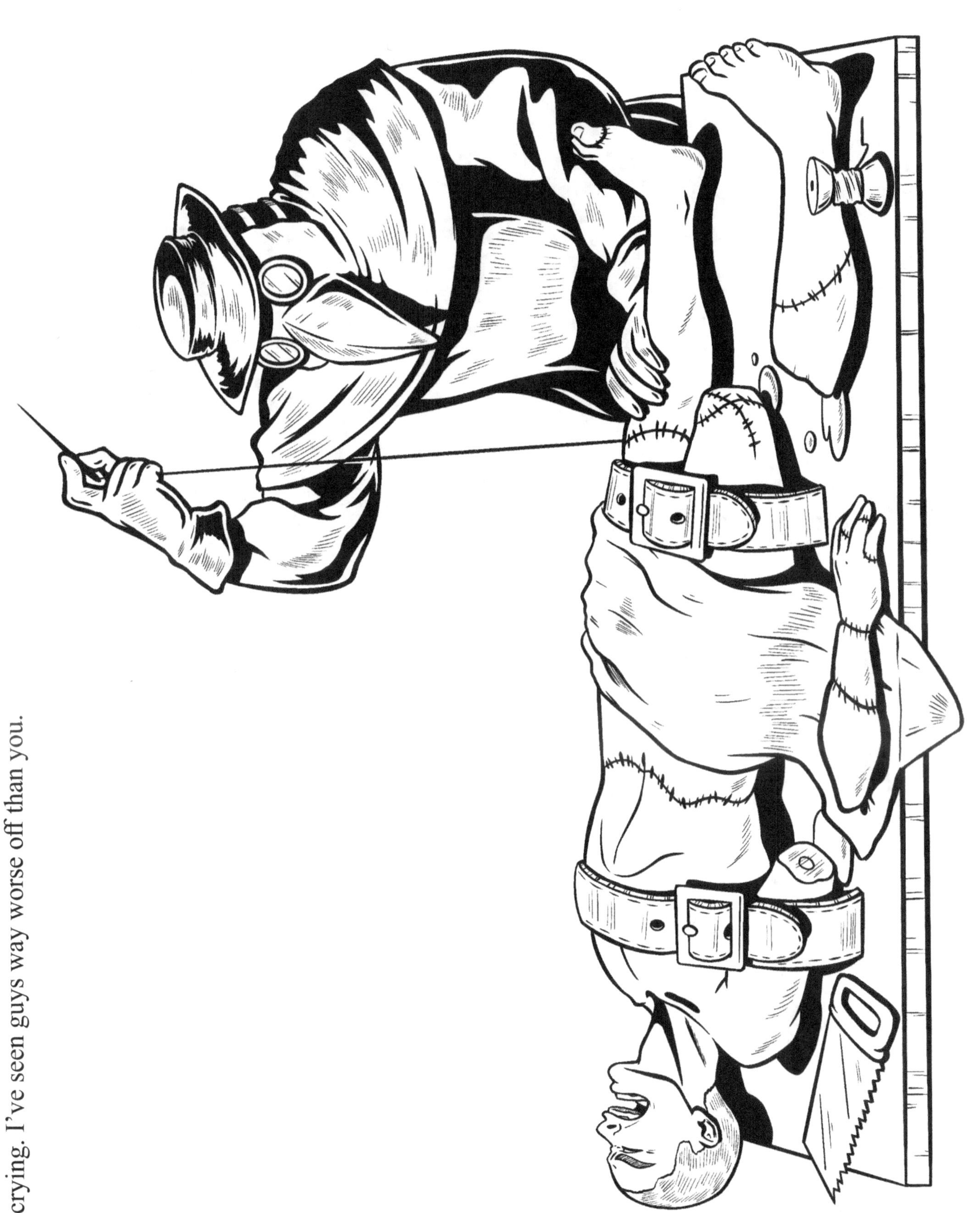

Stop crying. I've seen guys way worse off than you.

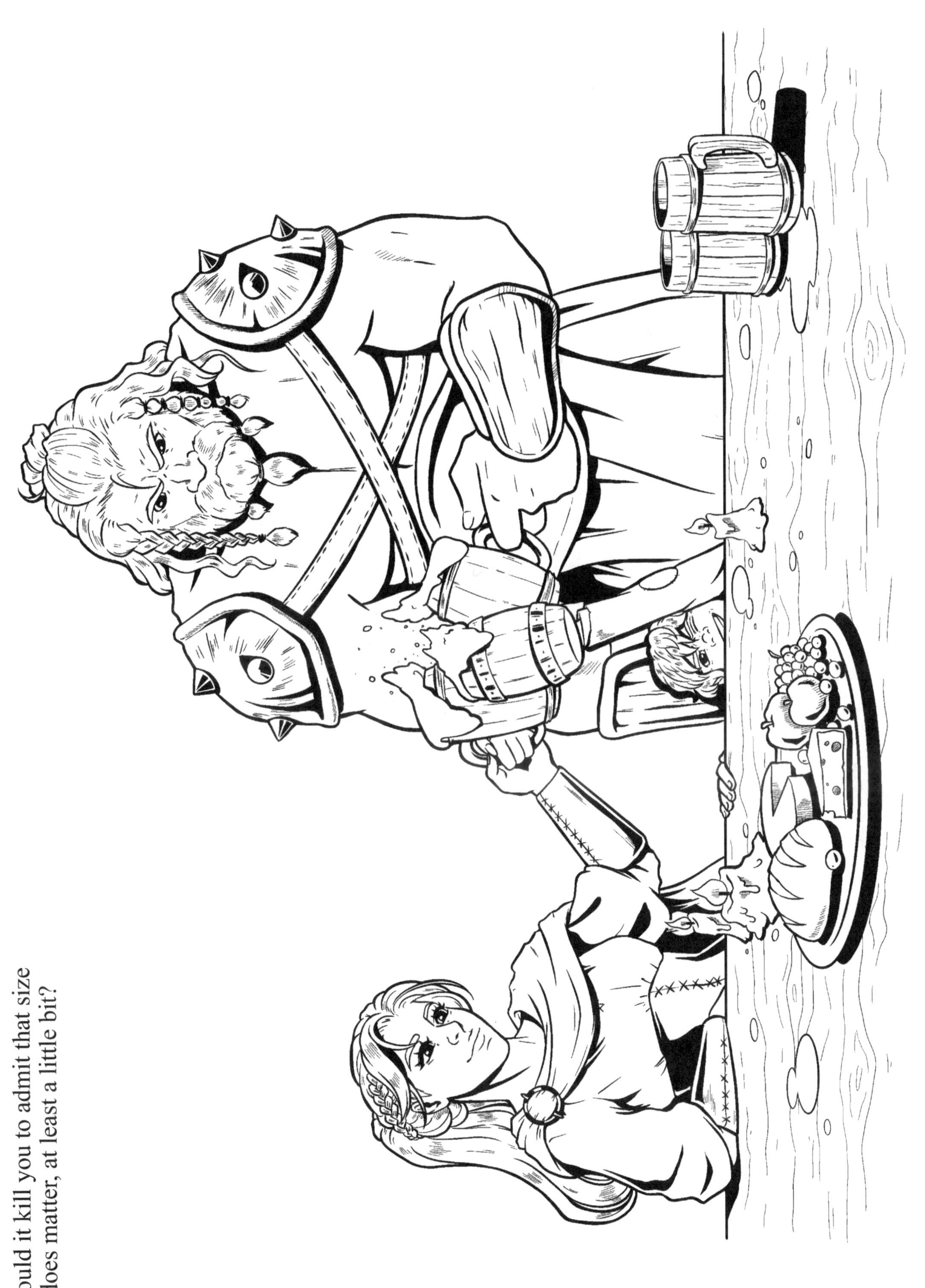

Would it kill you to admit that size does matter, at least a little bit?

Rats. Why does it always have to be rats?

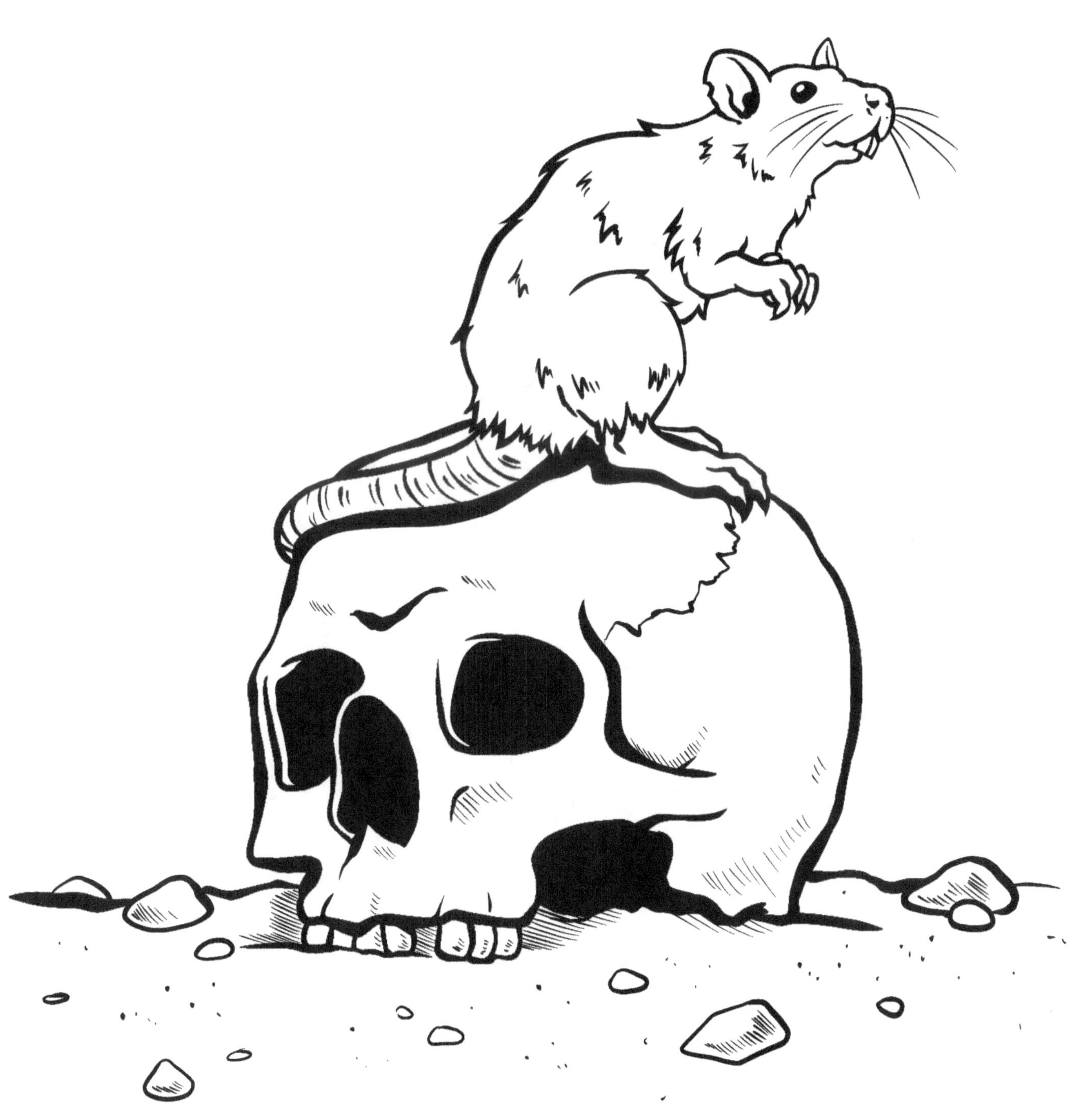

The streets are not kind to wagons. Let's just hope
this isn't another ambush.

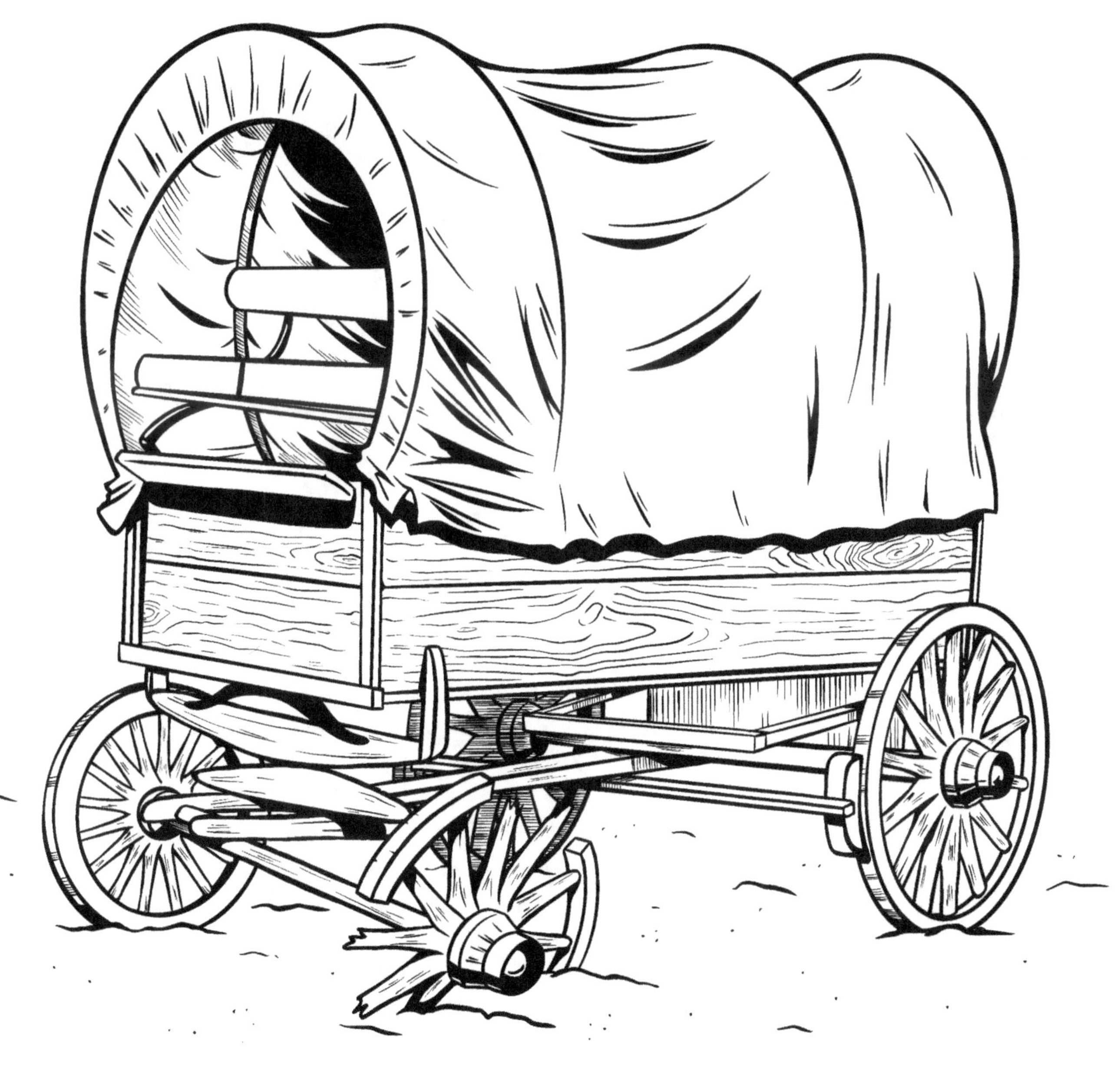

ZAYDEN

Zayden Joyner is a freelance artist and apiring game designer who loves building fantasy worlds, with the "help" of their pet cats. You can find more of their work on their website: zayden1.com

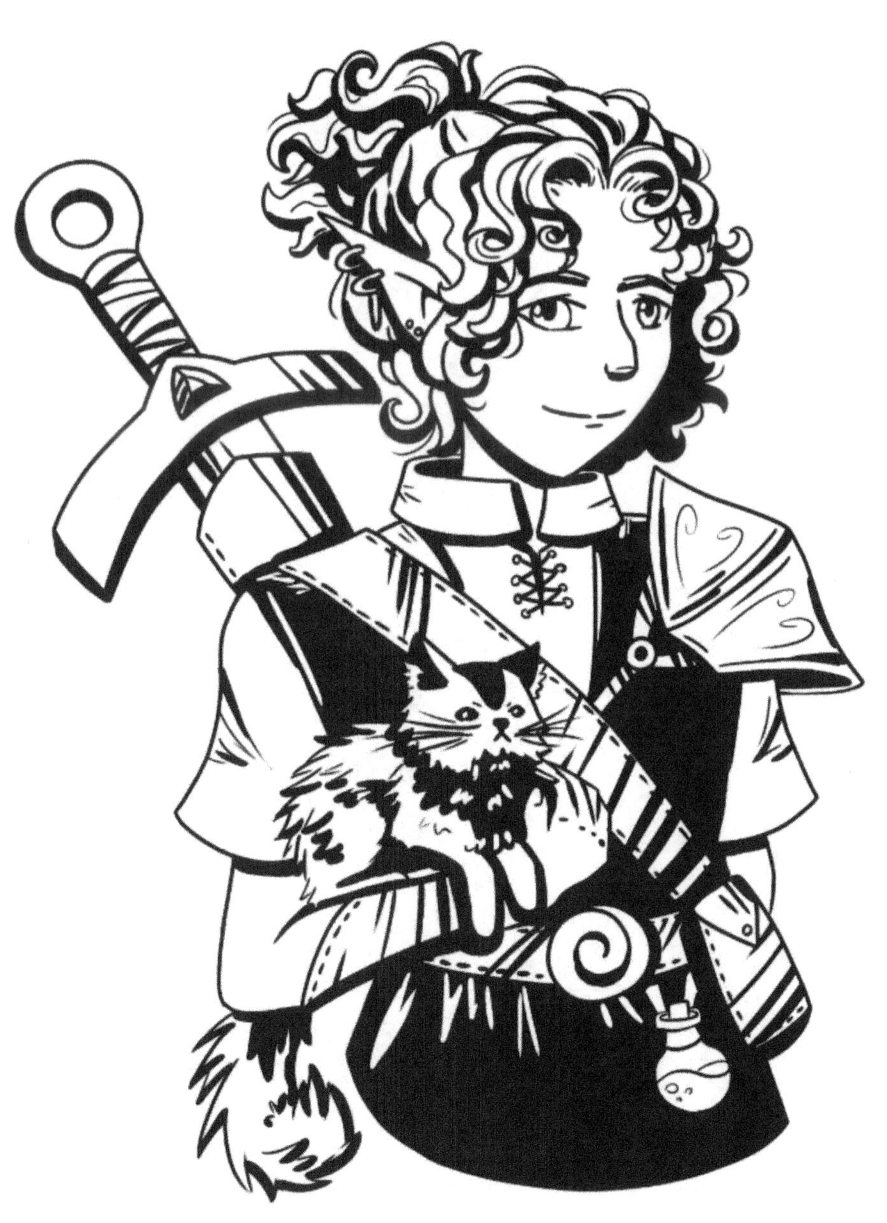

Be sure to drop by The Apple of your Pie bakery for a sweet treat!

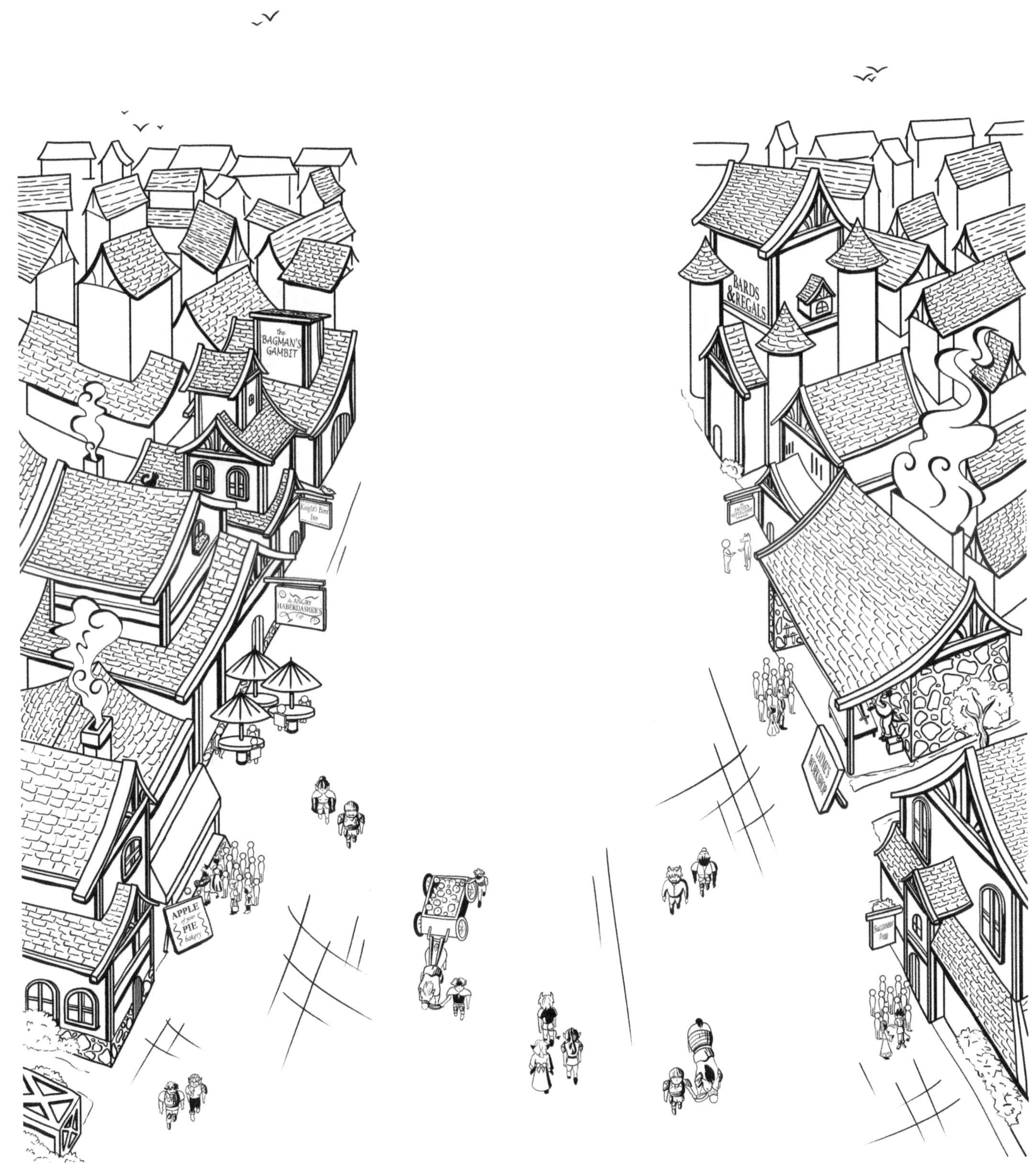

Evolution of the Hero

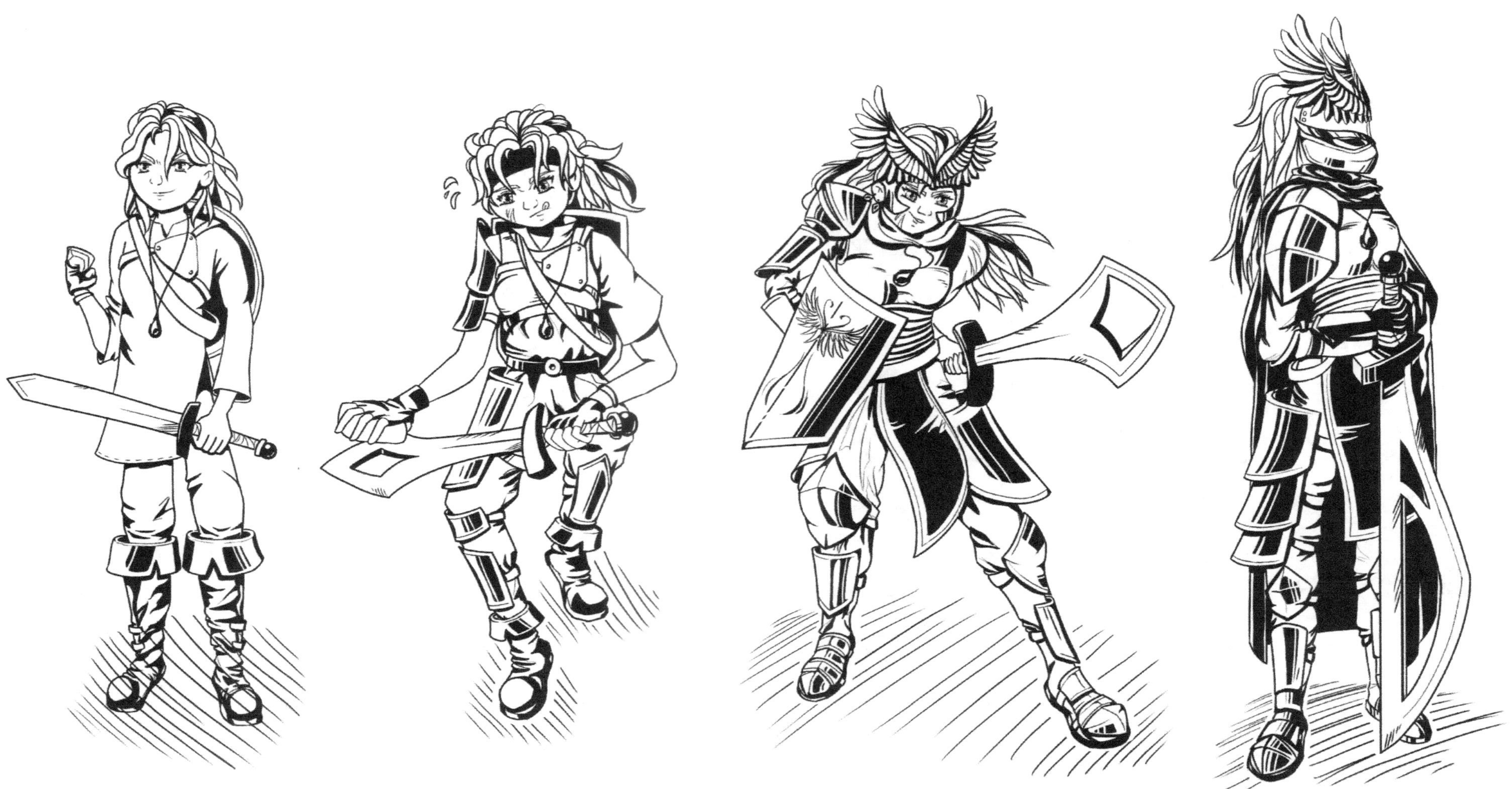

Just a boy and his giant magical hand, taking on the world.

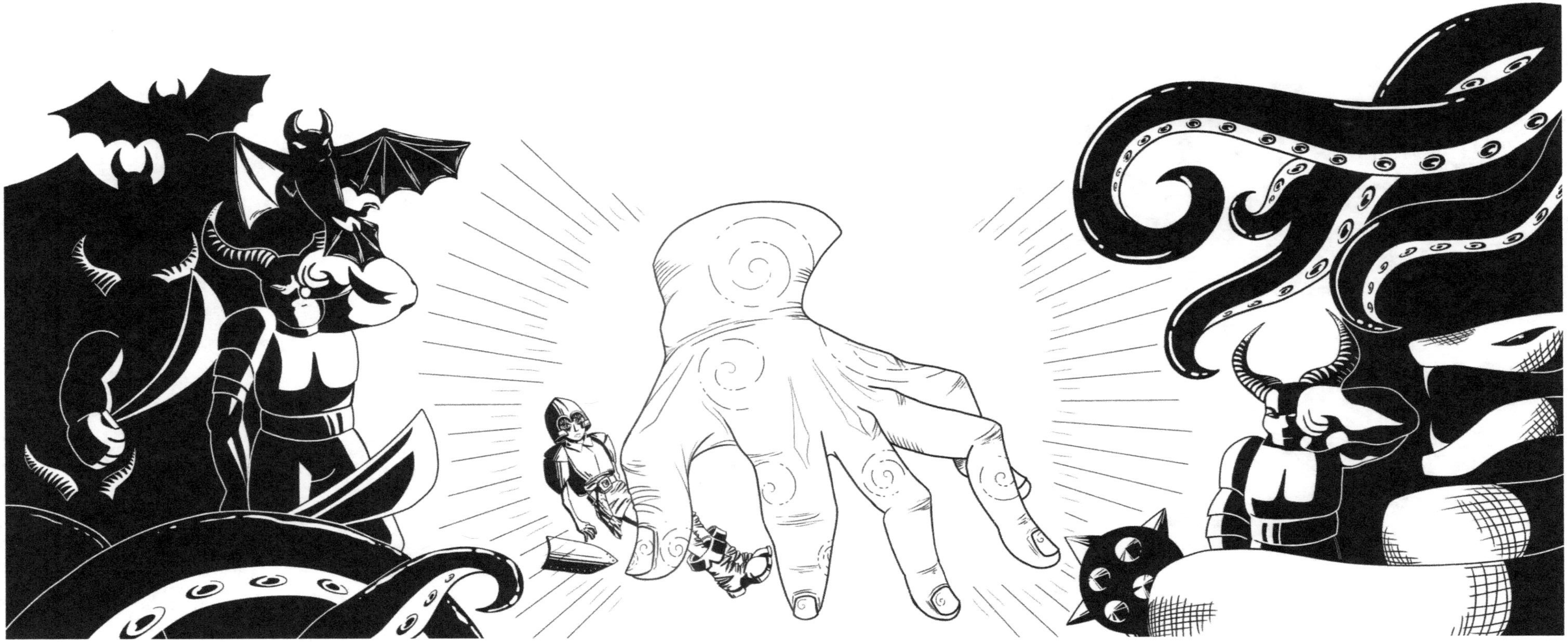

Five heads, oh is that all?

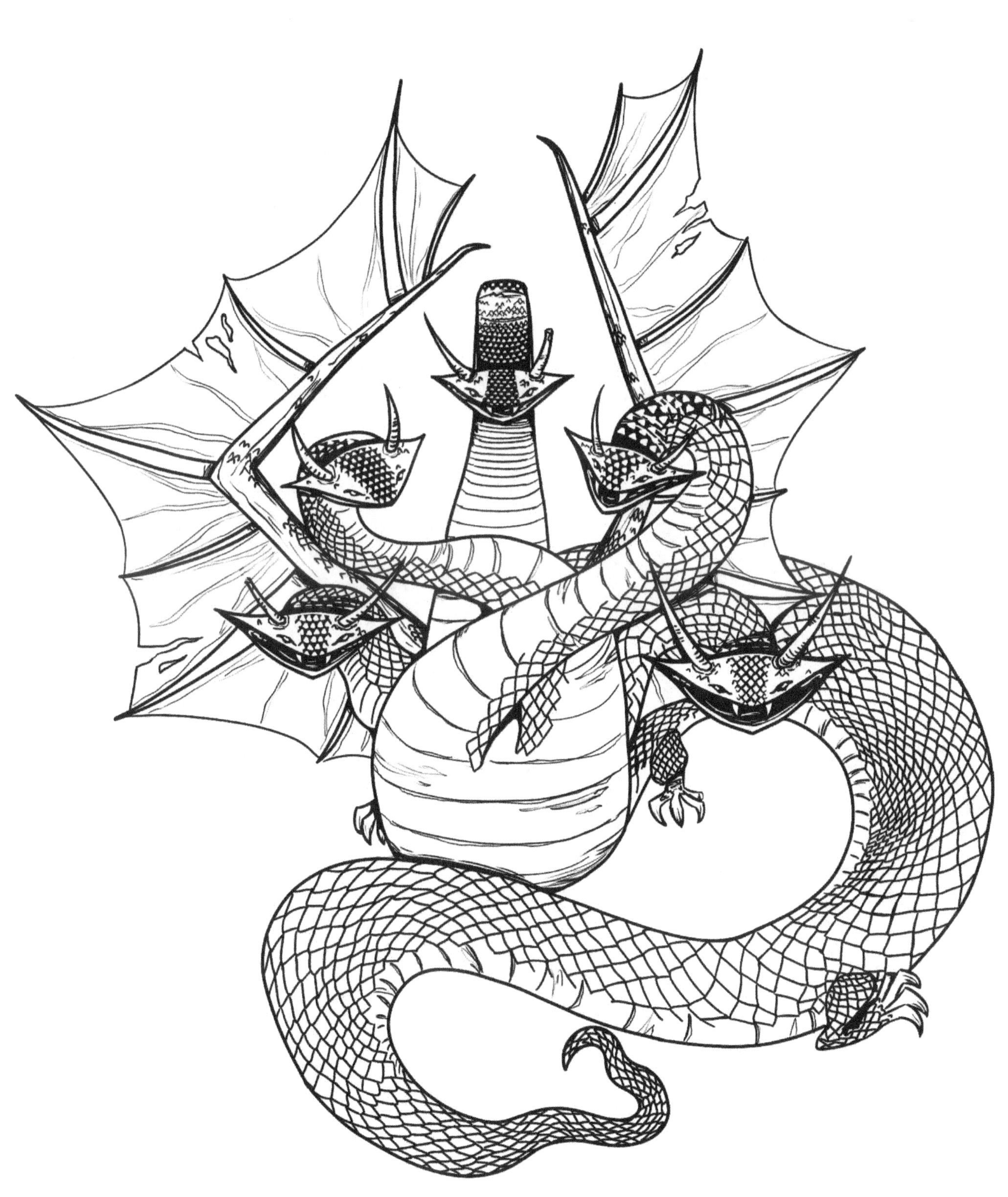

You never know what what flavor of treasures, or danger, you will find in the many ancient ruins that blanket the wilds of The Consortium.

In The City, beggars really CAN be choosers sometimes. So it would behoove you not to be too stingy when a gaunt man asks for a few Guilder.

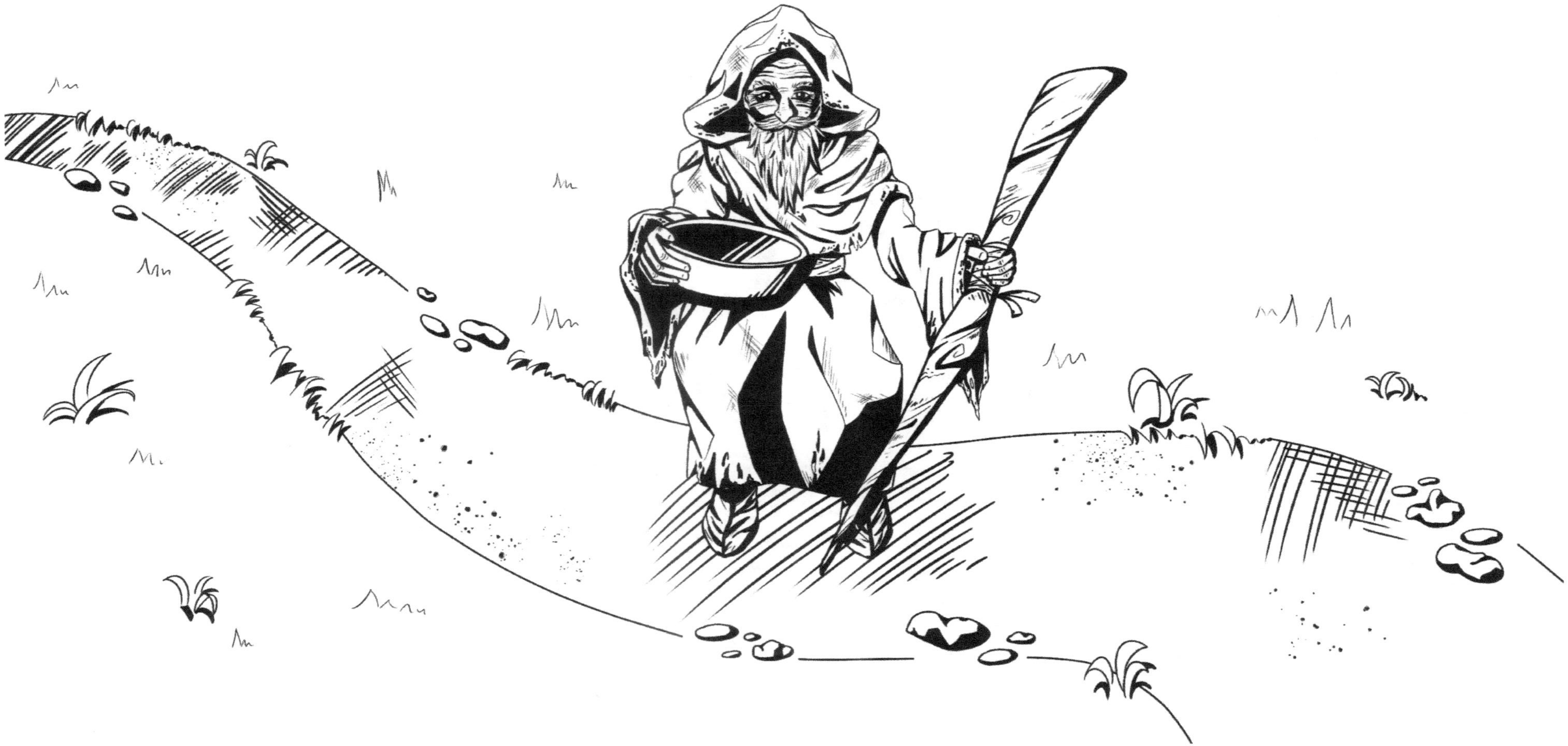

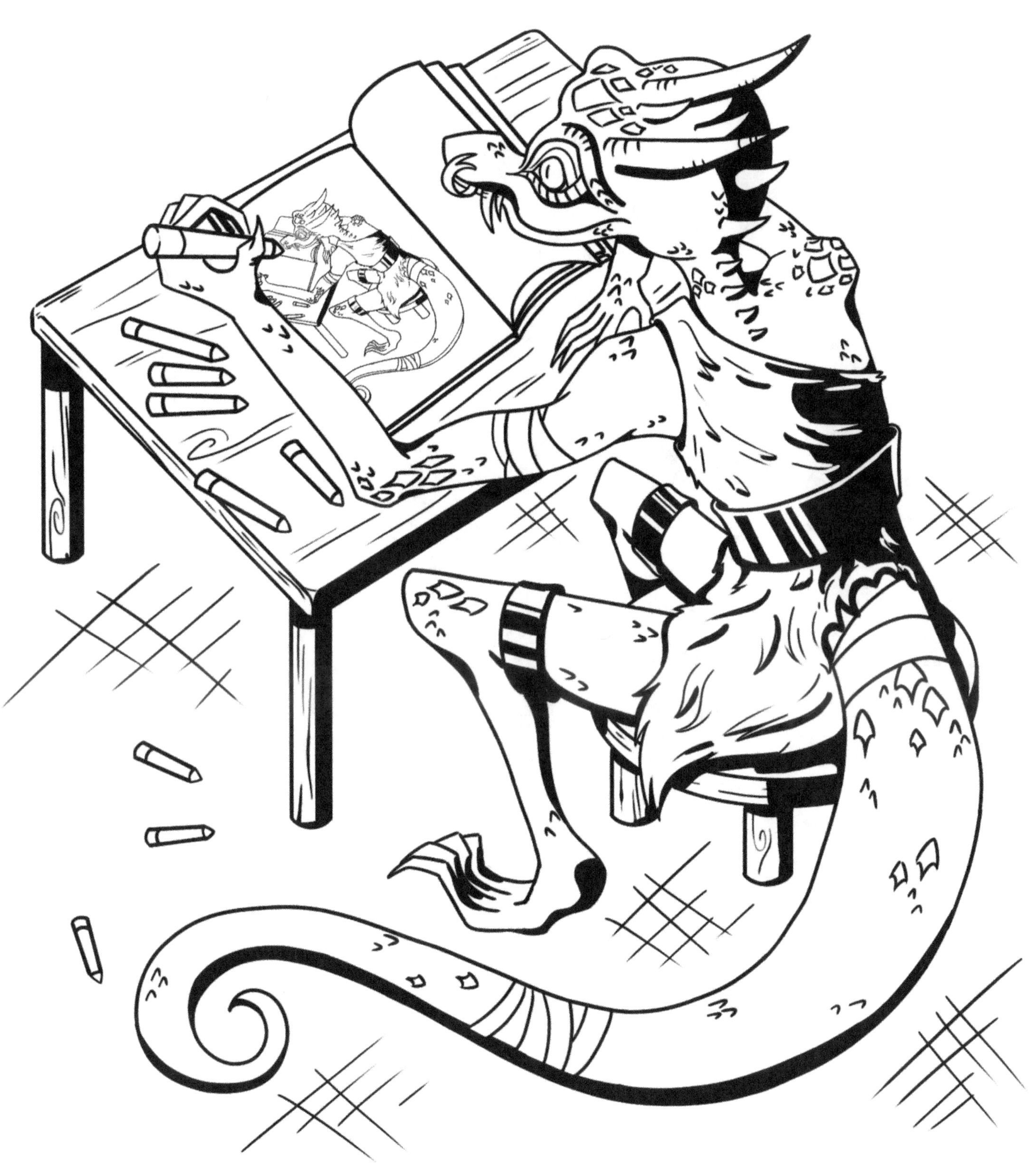